Praise for *Stay*

"The unconditional love of a pet, especially a dog, is the most remarkable of relationships. Combine that love with the ache of the inevitable circle of life and the realities of aging, and you have a story that goes deeper than the love of a pet. It is a larger tale of a bond that transcends the human condition, reaching the level of magic. Author Lisa Rimmert tells us a personal story of her own extraordinary connection with her beloved Dakota, a dog that will forever stay in her heart and the reader's too."

—David W. Berner, author of the bestseller
Walks with Sam

"Caring for an older dog can feel like a constant fight between your brain and heart: one aware of reality, and the other desperate to ignore it at all costs. Lisa Rimmert's tender and funny examination of this struggle will leave you teary-eyed, and extra appreciative that we're able to share any time at all with these incredible creatures. Our best friends. Our whole hearts."

—Kelly Conaboy, author of
The Particulars of Peter

"Even though many dogs come in and out of Rimmert's life, it's when the beloved Dakota is about to cross Rainbow Bridge the author speaks words that must jab even the hardest of hearts: 'I found myself begging the universe for time to slow down.' A heartfelt story to which many of us can relate, I must agree with the author on this one: companionship at its best is a dog."

—Elizabeth Moore Kraus, author of
3 Sisters. 3 Weeks. 3 Countries (Still Talking)

"A beautiful memoir that had me reaching for my two senior dogs to give them extra hugs and kisses. *Stay* will resonate with anyone who's had to say farewell to a beloved best friend."

—Victoria Schade, author of
Dog Friendly

D1596331

"*Stay* is a testament to love in all its forms. Rimmert's memoir is a profoundly human tale about how the bonds we form with our pets can prove to be just as precious and rewarding as those with our children. With lively colorful prose, *Stay* is an engaging, poignant love story."

—Rachel Michelberg, author of
Crash: How I Became a Reluctant Caregiver

"When our beloved dogs have come to the end of their roads, we are called upon to be at our most selfless, to put their peace and comfort above our own. I know from personal experience how excruciating it is to let go, but I doubt I could have written about it as beautifully."

—Peter Zheutlin, author of *The New York Times* bestseller
*Rescue Road: One Man, Thirty Thousand Dogs, and
a Million Miles on the Last Hope Highway*

STAY

STAY

My Forever Friendship with an Aging Dog

Lisa Rimmert

On The Nose, LLC
Middletown, DE

Cover design by Robin Ridley, parfaitstudio.com
Cover illustration by Rachel McGuire
Edited by Jennifer Huston Schaeffer, whitedogeditorial.com

First Edition
Printed in the United States of America

Published by On The Nose, LLC
Middletown, DE

ISBN 978-1-7368304-0-6 (paperback)
ISBN 978-1-7368304-2-0 (ebook)

"The truth is always somewhere in the middle."
—Charles William King, Jr.

In this book, you'll read *my* version of a real-life story, pieced
together from my perspective and memory, both of which are
limited. For narrative purposes, I chose to exclude some events and
to move others around in time. Some names and identifying
characteristics have also been changed. My hope is that I have
represented the heart of the story and the ordinary magic
of loving a senior dog.

For Brad

In a hundred ways, you made this story possible.
But, if you need to, you can put it in the freezer.

∞

An Accident

"Where's my Peepers?" I sang as I sauntered down the hallway toward the living room. Like most of the nicknames Brad and I had given Dakota, this one didn't mean anything. It was just something silly we'd called her once and it had stuck.

"Hey, hey, hey! Outside!" My voice lowered by two octaves and its volume went up threefold. I darted over to where Dakota was squatting, hooked my index and middle fingers under her collar, and whisked her out of the living room, through the dining room, and past the Christmas tree in the sunroom. "Let's go, let's go," I chanted while jogging beside her. The damage was already done, but rushing her outside felt like the right thing to do. I shut the door and turned around.

The poop stank. The voice from the webinar I'd been half watching blared at me from my laptop in the living room. I felt panicked—rushed. I couldn't think about what had just happened or what might've caused it. Not yet. First I needed to clean up the mess, to solve the problem. *Remove the poop, Lisa.*

I hurried back across the sunroom and into the kitchen to gather supplies: something to put it in and something to scrub the rug. I tore a poop bag from a roll in the basket on top of our fridge. I licked my fingertips and rubbed the end of the bag to open it like I'd done a thousand times—usually outdoors. *Paper towels? Under the sink.* I crouched in front of the cabinet and grabbed the roll. *Rug cleaner? Do we even have rug cleaner?* A vague memory of cleaning up Sidney's cat puke sprang to mind. Holding the cabinet doorknobs for balance, I pushed up to my feet and let the doors slam.

To my relief, a bright red bottle of rug cleaner stood out in the hall closet. *Good,* I thought. *I really didn't wanna go to CVS with poop residue lingering on my rug. This day has been stressful enough with work and now dealing with this accident. Why had Dakota even had an accident? Nope, not yet. Focus on the task at hand,* I told myself. *Remove the poop!*

I brought all of the supplies into the living room and held my breath while palming the poop with my bag-covered hand. The webinar yammered on even louder from the nearby coffee table. I exhaled slowly through my nostrils while twisting the end of the bag and tying it in a knot, then inhaled through my mouth and set the bag aside.

When I squeezed the trigger of the rug cleaner, only a little bit of liquid seeped from the nozzle. "Dah!" I exhaled in frustration. I adjusted the setting from STOP to SPRAY and spritzed it onto the carpet. *Success!* I skimmed the instructions, trying to find the number of minutes I needed to let the cleaner set, but I couldn't focus with the webinar going and my heart racing and Dakota waiting outside—possibly sick. *Whatever.* I tore off a few paper towels, crumpled them, and scrubbed.

Then, holding them poop side up, I looked around. *Whoops. Shouldn't have tied that bag yet.*

On my way outside, I snagged an empty plastic grocery bag from the basket on the fridge and dropped the paper towels into it. Holding the two bags, I slipped my feet into Brad's old pair of Vans and shuffled through the back door.

My panic subsided as soon as the door closed behind me, as if it magically shut out everything that had unnerved me. That was all *inside*: the poop smell, the webinar voice, the stress. Outside, I could breathe.

Dakota stood on the deck, watching me like she was curious what I was up to. Like she didn't just have an accident in the living room. Like everything was fine and dandy.

"Are you okay, puppy?" I scanned her face and body with my eyes, looking for any signs of distress. She looked completely normal—curious about my question but not upset, uncomfortable, or sick in the slightest. She turned to walk toward the grass like usual.

"Oh, so everything's fine?" I called after her with a sarcastic tone. I tossed the bags over the deck railing and watched them land next to the brown plastic trash can on the side of our house. *Gotta remember to put them in the bin later.* I breathed cool air into my lungs. The temperature was in the forties, chilly but sunny, average for a December day in Maryland.

"You just pooped inside but everything's fine?" I asked Dakota again, taking a seat on the edge of our big wooden deck, my feet resting on the patchy dirt and grass. Dakota stood an arm's length to my right, her nose wiggling as she took in the scents carried over from neighboring yards and the nearby woods. I squeezed my knees together and slid my hands between my thighs to warm them.

Dakota doesn't have accidents, I thought. *And yet, she just pooped on the rug right in front of me, like she couldn't help it.*

When I had walked down the hall to take a pile of folded laundry into the bedroom, I'd heard her behind me in the living room, rustling as she got up from her bed. I had assumed she was following me, but it turned out she was getting up to poop.

Did I forget to take her outside this morning? No, we went out before lunch. And if she needed to go out again, she would've let me know, I decided. *Even if she didn't ask me for some reason, she would've just held it.* Dakota hadn't peed or pooped inside since I house-trained her as a puppy—not even when she was alone for nine hours a day before I started working from home. *She's always been able to hold it. Something must be wrong.*

I wondered if I should take her to the vet. *She's acting fine, though. She's eating, drinking, in good spirits as always. No lethargy—no nothing. It's just this one accident. Maybe it's a fluke.*

That would be a pretty weird fluke, I debated with myself. *What logical explanation could there be other than some kind of medical issue? I should probably get her checked out just in case. I'd hate to assume it's nothing and be wrong. Right?*

I wasn't used to worrying about Dakota's health, and it wasn't a welcome feeling. I was much more comfortable thinking happy thoughts and assuming everything would always be okay. I like to think of myself as easygoing . . . laid back . . . not a worrier. That's why I've always resisted titles like "fur mom" and "pet parent." I'm nobody's mom, and I don't want to be. Moms have to fret over everything. *Is my kid safe and happy? Are they getting too much screen time? Am I hopelessly dorky for calling it "screen time"*? Mothering is a duty, a responsibility, and often a sacrifice. No thanks.

I preferred to think of myself as Dakota's friend. Friends go on adventures together. They have fun together. Dakota and I hiked, road-tripped, went to the dog park, played at the beach.... We did it all. Brad came along most of the time, but not always. Sometimes he was working, studying, or tired from working and studying. A couple of times, he was deployed overseas. Dakota and I were each other's constants.

"C'mere." I looped one finger under her faded red collar, and she sat by my side. Seated next to each other, I was only three inches taller than her. The fur on her muzzle, once black to match her nose and lips, had lightened to a mix of blonde and gray over our thirteen years together. It made her look earnest and wise, even after crapping in my living room.

Dakota weighed fifty-five pounds and had long limbs and a short but thick coat that blanketed everything we owned with dog hair. Twice a year, I could pinch sections of her undercoat and slide out tufts of fur between my fingers. Even though her coat began lightening up around age eight, I'd always considered her to be brown—specifically, golden brown, or fawn like a deer. I switched to calling her blonde after my friend Kim—who had two chocolate brown dogs—described Dakota that way. Kim was right: it fit better. Plus, I'd been dyeing my hair blonde for the past five years, and I liked that Dakota and I matched. We were two blonde peas in a pod.

I wrapped my arm around her neck and pulled her face to mine. She let me kiss her on the cheek but looked up and away, avoiding eye contact. Dogs don't roll their eyes, but if they did,

Dakota would've done it every time we subjected her to physical affection.

"You're silly," I said with a laugh. Then I moved my arm to give her space.

She stayed seated beside me, smelling the air. I actually loved that Dakota wasn't snuggly. She was strong and independent. We both were. Two blonde, adventurous peas in a pod.

I could've sat with Dakota on the deck until our toes froze, listening to the birds chirp and the breeze rustle the remaining leaves on the trees. But I knew my to-do list was growing longer by the minute, and I'd already lost some of my afternoon to the poop fiasco—not to mention that pointless webinar I felt like I had to watch because my boss, Mike, had suggested it. "Okay, puppy, let's go."

Inside, the webinar host droned on. Something about how important year-end fundraising is to nonprofit organizations. "No shit. Huh, Dakota?" *Ha! A pun. I kill me.* Without closing the computer, I picked it up along with a second pile of clothes and carried them down the hall to my office. Dakota followed. "Yeah, you *better* come with me, pooper," I joked.

I set my laptop on the desk and my clothes on the dresser, which I kept in my office since it didn't fit in our bedroom across the hall. When I sat down and woke up my computer, the monologue in my head immediately reappeared, loud and frantic. I was behind at work. *Beyond* behind. My unread emails and unchecked to-do list items stared me down like a lion preparing to tackle a gazelle. It made me feel hopeless, frozen in place.

It didn't help that I'd made my signature mistake that morning: looking ahead at my tasks list instead of just at the day's items. We needed to bring in $300,000 by the end of the year, but on December 10, 2018—with only twenty-one days to go—my thoughts kept trailing off from work to Dakota. I wanted to figure out if something was wrong with her, not think about fundraising.

Later, when I heard the beep of Brad's truck locking in our driveway, I hurried down the hall to the living room. Dakota followed me and then took the lead, galloping down the three wooden stairs to the small landing by our front door. With all the chaos earlier I hadn't stopped to text Brad, so I was eager to tell him what had happened. I wanted someone to share in the confusion I'd been feeling all afternoon. I also wanted his professional opinion about what the problem could be and what we should do to find out. Brad was a first-year physical medicine and rehabilitation resident at Walter Reed. I tease him that he's like a veterinarian but for humans, which is almost as good.

Head up and tail wagging, Dakota stood with Brad on the landing between the two front staircases of our split-level home.

"Hiya," I greeted him from the top of the stairs.

He slumped his right shoulder, letting his heavy black backpack fall to the floor with a thud. "Hi," he said with raised eyebrows, a dead giveaway that he'd had a stressful day too. I call it his version of an eye roll. He insists I'm making it up.

Keeping his shoulder lowered, Brad scratched the back of Dakota's neck. She graciously allowed him several seconds of affection before darting back up the stairs to find her favorite toy in the living room. With the bulbous rubber Kong in her mouth, she stopped at the top of the stairs and whipped it at Brad. It bounced off the middle step with a loud *clonk* and landed at his feet. Dakota waited, eager to see what he would do with it.

"Yes, hi, hello," Brad said to her as he picked up the Kong. Then, turning to me, he asked, "What's going on?"

I didn't usually greet him at the door, so he knew something was up. Most days, I remained shut away in my office when he got home. My job—raising money for an animal advocacy organization—was my passion. I often blurred the boundaries between work and "life." Brad would come home in the evenings, shedding a trail of items: backpack, wallet, keys, cell phone. Then he'd stop in the doorway of my office to say hello and tell me about his day, and that's when I'd realize I should quit for the day too—or at least take a break.

"We had an eventful day," I told Brad.

"Oh yeah?"

"Yeah! I made a doody!" I said, speaking in my "Dakota" voice. Brad and I started voicing Dakota's thoughts when she was a puppy—or what we *thought* were her thoughts. And what it might be funny if she *were* thinking. The voice we assigned her sounded youthful, high-pitched, and silly, like it belonged to a *South Park* character.

"Nice job." Brad smirked while hanging his keys on the caddy next to the door.

"No, I made a doody on the carpet!" I added on Dakota's behalf. Apparently, telling Brad simply that Dakota had defecated, without including the location, wasn't quite enough information to convey that there was a problem.

"What? For real?" Brad looked at me, his brow furrowed. *Now he gets it*, I thought. I switched to my regular voice. "Yeah, she pooped right here in front of me." I pointed to the rug.

"Hmm." The noise masked a swirl of questions. But before Brad could ask, I preempted a couple of them. "I took her outside just as much as I usually do. And she seems totally fine. I don't know what's going on."

Brad walked toward the kitchen, so I shuffled behind him and crossed through the room before stopping on the other side, in the sunroom. With its wood paneling painted light gray and its drop ceiling made of fake tiles, the room was obviously a later addition to the 1950s construction. It sits at the back of the house, behind the kitchen and dining room, accessible to both rooms through large doorways. It also leads to our backyard, so it sees a lot of traffic.

I leaned my butt against the pool table, which took up a good chunk of space in the room, and fidgeted with the bottom edge of the turquoise plastic cover that we kept on it in an optimistic yet somewhat ineffective attempt to protect it from pet hair. To my right, Dakota faced the kitchen and lowered her body to the carpet. Brad set her Kong on our tall black IKEA shelf, and Dakota's eyes followed his arm up, then down. I made a mental note to grab the Kong in a minute and put peanut butter inside it for her. I didn't dare speak those words in advance, though, at least not without using a code word. To keep Dakota from whimpering and following me impatiently, *Kong* was "K-word." *Walk* was "W." *Ride* was, regrettably, "R-word."

While Brad opened the fridge and pulled out food containers, Dakota watched his every move, her sweet, soulful eyes wide with hopefulness. As he carried ingredients from the fridge to the counter, one of his tattoos peeked out from his shirtsleeve, revealing my name, Lisa, inked on his muscular arm. I'd seen that tattoo a million times, but I still noticed it and thought about its origin story. We were engaged at the time, and when the tattoo artist found out that Brad was in the army, stationed far away from me and not yet married, he warned him, "Either marry her or break up now." I felt a twinge of smugness and pride reading my name on Brad's arm. We did get married, obviously, but we didn't do it because of external pressures. We did it because we wanted to—on our own terms and our own timeline. And there we were, still together fourteen years later. *In your face, tattoo guy.*

Brad's deliberate movements (and raised eyebrows—again) showed his distress. He was probably too worn out to contribute much to the conversation about Dakota's accident, but I didn't let that stop me from trying. When something's on my mind, I like to talk about it right away. I'm not great at waiting for the right moment.

"Do you think I should take her to the vet?" I asked.

Brad scrunched up his nose and rubbed his face with both hands, then slid them up through his short red hair. "It's definitely not normal for her to be pooping inside," he said, as if the answer was obviously yes.

"True," I agreed. I'd pretty much come to the same conclusion but needed reassurance.

Sidney appeared from the hallway, meowing as he sauntered through the kitchen, his belly swinging with each step. He was six or so and white all over except for the black fur covering his tail, the top of his head, and a few small spots on his legs. He slowed as he passed me, so I leaned far to my right to give him a quick scratch on his back. I slid my hand up his tail and held on for a second, pulling it slightly as he strolled out of reach. I liked that he wasn't a delicate cat. We're dog people, but we fostered Sidney in 2012. We officially adopted him a couple months later, after he proved himself to be easygoing, resilient, and, most importantly, as head over heels in love with Dakota as we were.

Sidney meowed again and paced in front of Dakota's face three times, displaying his hind end. Each time, she cricked her neck to keep his body from obstructing her view of Brad. Sidney took the hint and leaped onto the windowsill to scan the backyard for critters. Poor guy. Nobody was ever as interested in his butthole as he wanted them to be.

Brad assembled a wrap with veggie burger crumbles, tomatoes, peppers, hummus, mustard, and hot sauce.

"Condiment wrap?" I teased.

"Yes," Brad agreed, appeasing me. "Wanna watch an episode of *Better Call Saul* with me while I eat? Then I gotta work on my presentation."

"Sure," I responded. "I might order some Ethiopian food."

"Here," Brad said as he held out a chunk of tomato toward Dakota. She hurried over, nabbed it, and swallowed it without chewing. Then she looked to Brad for more. "All gone," he said, smiling. "Out of the kitchen."

Dakota backed up and lay with her body on the sunroom carpet and her front legs extending over the threshold into the kitchen. We had taught her the cue "out of the kitchen" several houses ago, and she understood its meaning in every one of them. She'd always cheat a little, though.

"Technically . . . ," Brad said in Dakota's voice. We both laughed.

I put peanut butter in Dakota's Kong, and the three of us went downstairs, where Brad and I watched TV from the futon. Dakota sprawled out on the carpet, blissfully licking peanut butter until none was left.

The next day, I made an appointment for her with the vet, who was able to see her later that week.

Goodbye #1

I have a faint memory of riding in the back seat of our family car in Texas when I was three years old. The memory is so fuzzy that I called my parents to see if it actually happened. They confirmed it was real. However, they've also been known to claim that I was a smartass as a child, so their opinions are obviously not to be trusted.

In the memory, my dad drove past some woods, talking with my mom, who was in the passenger seat. They were looking for a place to bury our puppy, Lucky. I don't remember my brother, Chip, being in the car, although he must've been. He would've been four at the time. Lucky didn't even make it to a year.

She had died after eating something poisonous. That's all I remember about her. Not her size. Not her personality. Not if the poison was in our yard or in a neighbor's. I don't know if she suffered. I don't even remember knowing her in real life—only through a picture I took out of one of my parents' old brown photo albums and held onto. The memories aren't there. I only recall feeling sad from the back seat of the car.

Just Arthritis

Brad lay on the rug in my office, resting after a workout in our basement gym. Nearby, Dakota posed like a sphinx, with her head up and front legs stretched out in front of her. It had been four days since her first accident and she'd had a second one two days after that.

I leaned back in my chair, which sat at a diagonal, and pushed back from my desk. I adjusted the bottom of my hoodie, flattening the protruding part so it wouldn't look like a kangaroo pouch. It was the second hoodie I'd worn that day; the first got covered in fur when I took Dakota to the vet's office that morning.

"Wha'd they say?" Brad reached above his head, feeling for Dakota's torso then scratching her side with both hands.

"He did a physical exam and asked me questions, but he couldn't find anything wrong with her," I reported to Brad. This was good news in my opinion. I didn't want unanswered questions, but I also didn't want anything to be wrong with Dakota.

"Huh," Brad said, then waited for me to continue.

"I guess it's just that the colder weather is making her arthritis hurt more than usual?" Even though that's precisely what the vet had told me, I wasn't comfortable phrasing it as a statement. Brad has vastly more medical knowledge than me, so I already felt insecure trying to relay the vet's words. I also worried that I hadn't asked enough questions or the right questions or that I'd translated things wrong from medical jargon to normal-people words. Brad's "huh" made me even more nervous.

Brad shifted onto his side to face me and bent one arm to support his head on his hand. His black workout pants swished against each other, and the torn sleeve of his ratty brown T-shirt flopped over toward the floor.

I thought about making a joke by lunging toward him and pretending to rip it off, but I picked at the tip of my fingernail instead. "The vet said dogs with arthritis will sometimes avoid going outside when it's cold. Then they wait too long to poop and can't hold it in."

Dakota had been diagnosed with arthritis at her first so-called "senior dog" checkup in Denver in 2014. During a physical, the vet stretched one of Dakota's back legs out behind her to assess its range of motion, and the action made Dakota yelp. If I hadn't already wanted to punch the vet for calling Dakota a "senior," I would have for causing her pain. The vet assured me Dakota's reaction was typical in "senior dogs" (that's three punches she deserved, if you're counting), so she prescribed carprofen—a nonsteroidal anti-inflammatory drug, or NSAID—to help with the inflammation in Dakota's hips. She also recommended a joint supplement, which didn't seem to help, but Dakota liked the taste of it so we gave it to her almost every day.

"That sounds like a cop-out," Brad scoffed. "It's *cold* outside, so all of a sudden she starts pooping in the house?" He furrowed his brow.

Humph.... I guess my answer wasn't satisfactory. I shifted my eyes away from his, not sure how to respond. Sometimes he seemed to argue just to argue. I was sure his comment was directed at the vet, not at me, but I couldn't help but take it personally. It felt like he was questioning *me* and my intelligence. I tried to find something else to focus on—a reason for not looking at Brad. Across the room, my closet overflowed with clothing that didn't fit in my tiny bedroom closet across the hall. Beneath the clothes sat a bunch of papers and photos: stacks of flyers, newsletters, and envelopes for my job, as well as two plastic tubs of old report cards ("doing well but too chatty"), materials from my professional portfolio (marketing samples and newspaper clippings from columns I penned about animal welfare), and old film photos (childhood friends, family, and dogs I once knew and loved). The walls and shelves of my office were decorated with feminist- and animal-themed art: a yellow wooden cutout of the words "Nevertheless, she persisted" and figurines of an elephant, a frog, and a couple of dogs. On my desk laid a pad of yellow sticky notes. I swiped it and watched each sheet separate as I shuffled the edge with my thumb.

"I don't buy that she's had two accidents in the house because it's a little colder outside," Brad continued.

I still didn't answer. Instead, I looked at Dakota. When our eyes met, she stood and shuffled her feet. *Good, a distraction . . .*

an excuse to exit. I needed a break, and I also knew from experience that Brad is better at communicating once he gets a moment alone to process things.

"Wanna go outside?" I asked Dakota in a singsong voice. When she shuffled again, I said to Brad, "Let me take her out real quick." I closed my laptop and stood, stretching my arms over my head and yawning. Dakota followed me down the hall, and Brad walked behind her. She and I passed through the kitchen, where Brad stopped to look in the snack cabinet. "B-R-B," I called to him from the back door.

"B-R-H," he replied.

Dakota peed then lingered, sniffing the grass. I crossed my arms and meandered around the deck, watching her and enjoying the outdoors. I loved our backyard. It was bigger than you'd expect for the DC suburbs, and the tall trees lining our fence made me feel like we were in our own little world. That feeling got interrupted occasionally by the sound of a nearby leaf blower or the neighbor kids shouting over the fence at us from their big, obtrusive trampoline. But, for the most part, it was my happy place. This house was the ninth place we'd lived with Dakota and only one of three with fenced-in yards, so I treasured it.

As I watched Dakota explore, I thought about Brad's reaction to what I'd told him the vet said. *I don't know why he's pushing back on it. I've heard of cold weather causing arthritis flare-ups, and it* had *been chilly lately. Plus, I trust the vet.* We'd gone to this vet for Dakota and Sidney since moving to Silver Spring the previous year. He always seemed kind and knowledgeable, and he looked and sounded like Zach Braff, who'd played a doctor on TV. Enough said.

I liked Dr. Braff's theory that the weather caused Dakota's accidents—that her arthritis caused them. That was something I could manage by being more proactive about taking her outside, instead of waiting for her to tell me she needed to go. *It'll be easy since I work from home,* I assured myself. *I can take her out ten times a day if I need to. No problem.* Looking back, I know that I was so quick to accept the vet's suggestion because it shielded me from having to consider any causes that might've been more complex, serious, or persistent. Luckily, Brad had more clarity.

I hugged my arms closer as a breeze came through, but I endured the chill to give Dakota ample time in case she needed to poop. *See? I'm already nailing this.* When we went back inside, Brad was sprawled out on the sunroom carpet, just outside the kitchen. He rested his chin on his forearm as he watched a clip from a late-night talk show on his iPad.

"Anyway," I said, continuing our conversation, "I think I can just do a better job of taking her outside more often." I sat next to him, cross-legged and self-assured.

He paused his video and asked, "What about a specialist? Whatever happened to that discussion?"

Oh, yeeeah. Months earlier, Brad and I had batted around the idea of finding a specialist for Dakota to see if they could slow the progression of her arthritis or even reverse it. So far, her case was mild. She got up from lying down a little slower than she used to, but she got around just fine. She ran, she jumped, she played. But I knew arthritis gets worse over time, so if we could change that, I definitely wanted to.

"I forgot about that," I said. "I haven't found anyone." I liked the idea of going to a specialist, I just hadn't done the research yet. It hadn't seemed urgent, so I'd figured we would look for someone when Dakota got a little older. I'd told Brad that we'd "cross that bridge when we come to it," a phrase I employed when I wanted to avoid dealing with something—like Dakota getting older.

With Dakota's recent accidents, though, I could see that this might be a good time to take her to a specialist. If Dr. Braff was right about arthritis being the cause of her accidents—and I thought he was—maybe a specialist could do something about it, like slow it down or even do some cool antiaging procedure with stem cells.

"Well, I'm sure there's a specialist around here," Brad said sharply, like if there wasn't, he'd be calling our congressperson and lodging an official complaint. He flipped his iPad so it was facing him vertically, as if he was about to do a Google search.

"No, I just mean that I haven't looked. I can find one. Let me find one."

"Okay." Brad pushed his iPad away, keeping his arm extended on the carpet. Dakota lay nearby with her head up, probably wondering why neither of us had made ourselves useful and gotten her a treat.

"What kind of specialist does arthritis stuff?" I asked Brad.

"Physical medicine. Like me, but for dogs." In his job at Walter Reed, Brad saw patients with all kinds of musculoskeletal problems, including chronic back and joint pain, as well as brain and spinal cord injuries.

"Gotcha." I turned to Dakota. She looked at me, the nearby treat cabinet, then back at me. When I stood up, she watched my hands as I grabbed a treat bag and unsealed it. She sat down before I had the chance to ask her to. She licked her lips and looked at me with wide eyes. I put my hand out in front of my body, palm facing her, like I was a traffic cop telling her to stop.

"Stay," I instructed as I pulled out a treat then took three steps backward and waited a few seconds.

"Okay," I said to both Dakota and Brad. Dakota bolted over, took the treat from my hand, and lay down to chew it on the sunroom carpet.

"I'll do some googling tomorrow," I continued, only to Brad.

"Cool," he replied, smiling and fixing his eyes on Dakota. As she finished licking the last crumbs from the carpet, he rose to his knees and fists, like a gorilla, and stared intensely at Dakota. I smiled when I saw his movements, happy to see him being silly.

"Uh-oh, Dakota. Watch out," I warned her playfully.

She stood and watched as Brad began lifting and dropping his fists to the floor, as though he were stalking her.

"Rooh!" she barked and shuffled backward.

Brad crawled toward her and chased her around the pool table. While Dakota ran, he plodded behind her, moving much more slowly on all fours than she did. When she made it back to her original spot by the entryway to the kitchen, she paused to look at me, then the treat cabinet, then back at me.

I burst out laughing. "Okay, I played with Brad. Can I have another treat now?" I said in Dakota's voice.

"What?!" Brad squawked. "Ridiculous."

I gave her another treat.

That night, unable to fall asleep, I looked online and found a specialist clinic in a town thirty minutes north of us. They did sports medicine, rehab, regenerative medicine, and more, and their reviews were positive. The next day, I scheduled an appointment for January—the soonest opening they had. I also found out we'd need to bring an X-ray of Dakota's hips, so I made an appointment with Dr. Braff to have that done too. I slept well, confident in our plan to address Dakota's arthritis.

Hello

The first time I laid eyes on Dakota was in 2005. She was just a pixelated image on the Internet. The puppy in the picture was so perfect for me that if I'd been on an online dating site, I might've thought I was being catfished. It was like the picture had been planted online by a creepy, yet skillful, middle-aged man with a thing for dog-loving twentysomethings. But I wasn't looking for a romantic partner; I already had one of those. I was looking for something even more important: a dog.

Brad was at work, and I was still in my light blue fleece pajama pants in our second bedroom, which we used as an office and a storage area for Brad's army gear.

Brad had rented the apartment for us earlier that year. He had already been living in Fayetteville, North Carolina, for the last couple of years, and after our wedding, I moved down from Illinois. Barely an adult, I had just finished undergrad, which is the word I use instead of *college* because I want you to know that

I also have a graduate degree now. I need to get something out of that $36,000 certificate, even if it's only bragging rights.

At the time, Brad had been accepted to study Arabic at a school in California, so we knew we'd be moving again in October. His job in the army had already sent him overseas a few times, and return trips were on the horizon. This was the perfect time for him to attend the school because it would give us an uninterrupted year and a half together as newlyweds.

Since we'd only be in Fayetteville for a few months, we didn't bother settling in. I left most of my belongings at my parents' house in Illinois, to be picked up on our way to California. I also didn't bother looking for a job there. Instead, I holed up in our apartment, scouring the Internet for a dog to adopt. That was my job. I was the CEO of finding cute puppies, and I was great at it.

I sat down at the desk and jiggled the mouse to wake up our computer—the old-school kind with a separate tower and a monitor that juts out ten inches in the back. Then I clicked on the address bar and typed:

www.petfinder.com

Petfinder is the go-to website when you're looking to adopt a pet. You get to choose from all kinds of criteria, including location, breed, age, and even whether a dog gets along well with other dogs. I had been a fan of the website since I'd first learned about it while working at an animal shelter during my undergrad years.

When I started looking for a dog to adopt, pit bulls were at the top of my list. At the shelter, I had seen firsthand how misunderstood they are. Some people think they are naturally prone to aggression, present a danger to children, or can lock their jaws when they bite. None of that is true. Pit bulls *are* known for their tenacity. But, like all dogs, they're products of their training. So a pit bull's tenacity can show up as determination in a dogfight, if that's the behavior a person has taught the dog to exhibit, or it can show up as incessant kissing and tail wagging, which is what I saw from the pit bulls I'd met at the shelter.

I wanted to adopt a sweet little pittie and prove all the naysayers wrong. My mom's response to that sentiment was, "Lisa, please don't," which just made me want one even more. I'm a little rebellious—or, if you ask my mom, a *lot* rebellious.

Fortunately for my mom, I didn't have much luck. At the time, North Carolina had one of the worst records for abuse and neglect of pit bulls, so shelters and rescue groups had extra safeguards in place to protect them. People who run rescue groups mean well, but sometimes they can go too far with these types of safeguards, making it hard for good, caring people (*ahem!*) to adopt dogs. I've seen blanket requirements for things like homeownership, fenced-in yards, and previous ownership of a specific dog breed. It always seemed bananas to me that a shelter would rather keep a dog in a kennel with no exercise than let them live with a family who—*gasp!*—rents an apartment.

Now, with my experience working in animal rescue, I could've talked my way into the staff's good graces without a hitch, yard or no yard. They just wanted to hear the same thing I would've wanted to hear: "We've already cleared this with our landlord, and we'd be happy to have anyone from the rescue group drop in to do a home check." But there was a bigger problem: pit bull rescue groups were also requiring that the shelter staff choose which family could adopt which dog. Other than wanting a pit bull, I didn't have specific preferences for age, size, or color—but I did feel strongly about being allowed to choose which dog I felt a connection with. My doggy, my choice.

So, as the CEO of finding cute puppies, I made an executive decision to broaden my search to include shepherd, Lab, and hound mixes. These dogs were really my type anyway. I'm not sure what first drew me to them as a child, but I like these breeds now because they're unpretentious. They're just dogs—smart, silly, uncomplicated dogs. They're commonly seen in shelters, and they don't typically get oohs and ahhs from people like so-called designer breeds do. I like an underdog and I like to go against the grain. When I see a person walking with two dogs—one who appears to be a mixed breed and one who looks like a designer breed—I always make a point to compliment the mixed breed dog a little more. I figure the *-oodles* and *-doodles* and *-poos* get enough attention.

While I scanned and clicked through Petfinder, one picture caught my attention. Like a reflex, my finger lifted off the computer mouse and my hand froze in place. My eyes jumped from the photo to the description:

Betsy
Female
Four months old

It's rare to get much more than the basic info when you're looking at young puppies who haven't been at the shelter for long. The staff hasn't had time to learn about their personalities. But that was enough information for me. I was in love.

I studied Betsy's picture. She faced the camera, but her gaze was focused on something off to the right. She rested her two front paws on an object in front of her, which was covered by a green towel. It blocked her hind legs and the rest of her body, so the only things exposed in the picture were her face, neck, and front legs. Betsy's nails pressed into the towel-covered object, as if at any moment she might press harder for leverage and launch over it, barreling into the camera's tripod.

Dark green vines and leaves formed the photo's backdrop. It brought out the color of Betsy's rounded head. She had golden brown fur—like a little deer—with a black muzzle that camouflaged her nose, which was also black. One of her ears flopped forward, while the other stood half erect. Her eyebrows looked like two charcoal smudges smeared up from the inside corner of each eye.

Betsy's curious expression and smudgy black eyebrows captivated me. They reminded me of a dog I'd had as a kid. I right-clicked on Betsy's face and saved the image to my computer so I could show Brad when he got home from work. It was the only picture I'd saved during my search for a dog.

I called the shelter to make sure Betsy was still available for adoption, and the file—"Betsy.jpg"—waited on my desktop until Brad got home from work that evening. I convinced him we should go visit her, using the phrase, "Come on, we'll just go see her." In hindsight, I understand that I was being manipulative. But I've never been less sorry.

Three days later, Brad and I met Betsy in a small office at the animal shelter. Our encounter was different than I had expected. This puppy didn't bound over to us and lick our faces. She didn't playfully tug on anyone's shoelaces. She approached me and then Brad, but she didn't stay long enough for any face licking or shoelace tugging. Instead, she seemed independent, almost aloof, making a beeline from person to person and smell to smell. She didn't stick around at any of her stops; she got distracted almost immediately by the next sight or scent. I loved her silliness, her energy, her confidence. Brad seemed to get a similar kick out of her antics.

As my eyes darted around the room, following Betsy's movements, I beamed like a child. I had always dreamed of having a dog of my own, and here she was. My life was going to take me on some cool adventures, and this puppy seemed like the perfect copilot.

Brad and I stepped outside to talk. He lit up a cigarette as soon as we were through the door. I anxiously bit at my thumbnail.

"I want her!" I blurted out. Adopting a dog was one of several huge, life-altering decisions I've made without taking time to weigh the pros and cons. They were just givens. I graduated high school and went to college—not because I knew what career I wanted and college was the pathway to achieving it, but because college is just what you do after high school. I never questioned it.

After college, I got married, not questioning that either. Brad had been my boyfriend through senior year of high school and all of undergrad. I loved him and we would talk about getting married one day, so when he asked me, I said yes.

Actually, I said no the first time but not because I didn't want to marry him. I just felt too young to be engaged then and wasn't ready to say yes. It wasn't so much a "no" as it was a "try again in a year or two." I'm lucky he did.

"What do you think?" I asked Brad in front of the animal shelter.

He responded with math. While I was thinking about all the fun we'd have with Betsy—the walks, the tricks I'd teach her, the laughter she'd bring us—Brad considered the financial responsibilities.

He'd been managing his own money since he was thirteen years old and got his first job mowing lawns in Mascoutah, Illinois, his small hometown about thirty miles east of St. Louis, Missouri. He'd bought his own TV and VCR, then later his own car, gas, and cigarettes.

I, on the other hand, received a weekly allowance from my parents well into my high school years, and even though I had summer jobs, they paid for gas, clothes, and pretty much whatever else I wanted. I drove hand-me-down cars from my parents or brother, and, in undergrad, my dad would pass me a five-dollar bill every weekend when I came home to do laundry. At age twenty-one, I had to empty out my checking account to buy Brad a simple, gold wedding band for $200. Bottom line: he was much more grown up than I was.

At the shelter that day in August 2005, Brad ran through some calculations too quickly for me to follow, figuring up approximately how much money it would cost each year to care for a dog, including food and vet visits.

"Yeah," he said, comfortable with the total he came up with. "Let's do it."

"Are you sure?" I hesitated. I couldn't accept his answer at face value. I think I recognized that I had asked him to make a commitment with me before thinking it through enough to be sure I was ready for it too. I was impulsive. I'd gone through life relying on people more discerning than me to slow things down and consider the pros and cons of *my* decisions. So when Brad quickly said yes to adopting Betsy, I needed to be the one to slow things down. For me, adopting a dog would be an unbreakable commitment. If we signed the papers to add Betsy to our family, I was going to keep her until the very end, no matter what. I was going to do this the right way. I needed to consider that—and make sure Brad understood and was okay with it too.

"You understand it's forever, right?" I asked. "Like, no matter what happens, I'm not giving her away. Even if we end up homeless and starving, I'll feed her my last french fry from the dumpster. I'm not giving her up."

I bit my thumbnail while I awaited Brad's response.

He didn't need the clarification. He knew how I felt about animals. Because he's a planner, he had probably considered the long-term nature of this decision before he'd ever agreed to go with me to the animal shelter. And he was on board. "Of course it's forever," he said. "If you want the puppy, let's take her home."

When I want something complicated, expensive, or cumbersome, Brad has this amazing way of making it seem easy. When I wanted to do improv and stand-up comedy in my twenties, he said, "Do it!" After we'd moved to Colorado and I was going to miss out on the improv festival my friends were hosting in St. Louis, he insisted that I buy a plane ticket and attend. When I was thinking of leaving a well-paying job I'd only worked at for a year to take a lower-paying position in animal advocacy, Brad was all for it—even as I skipped through our house, saying, "I'm thirty and I already have my dream job!" while he was in the thick of medical school and working tirelessly toward his own dream. I can't remember a time when I haven't had his wholehearted support in pursuing my passions. That's one of my favorite things about him.

As we stood outside the animal shelter, Brad held his cigarette to his lips and sucked in one last time. He pressed the end of it between his thumb and index finger until the ashy tip fell to the ground, then he stepped on it with the toe of his new Vans. He flicked the cigarette butt into the trash can and held the door for me to enter. "Let's go get her."

Back inside, I filled out the adoption application with the usual information: name, address, phone number, yada, yada. Then I read a question that to most people would be insignificant: Under what circumstances would you consider surrendering the animal?

The options included moving, divorce, and allergies, and I had to circle the ones that would make me consider returning Betsy. I left all of them as is and wrote in big letters at the bottom: N/A.

Brad and I bought puppy supplies and waited with excitement for three days for Betsy to be spayed so she could come home. We decided on a new name for her—one that Brad remembered from a comic book he'd read when he was little. It was called *Wild West C.O.W.-Boys of Moo Mesa*, and the namesake bull in the story was the Dakota Dude.

"Dakota, c'mere! Dakota, stay!" It was perfect, and so was she.

Christmas

Fundraising professionals are bound to get a few rude emails on Christmas Day. We also get kind ones accompanied by generous donations, but the mean ones stand out more.

Reclining against the armrest of the love seat with my laptop perched on my stomach and thighs, I read the latest email a second time:

> Don't ever email me again. UNSUBSCRIBE.

"Could you not find the unsubscribe link in the very email you're replying to?" I said to the computer screen, rhetorically asking the sender of the email. Some people behave as if their emails don't come from actual people. I was the person behind our organization's fundraising emails, and I had begun to dwell on the mean responses, taking them personally even though I knew I shouldn't. I'd get defensive, though only in my head or while venting to my coworkers—never to members of the public. The closest I ever came to that was sending *super nice* emails full of sarcasm that I knew the recipient would read as sincerity. "I'm *so glad* you reached out about this *important* problem. I'd be *delighted* to get it resolved for you!"

"Dakota, do you wanna go to the park?" I asked her.

Her head popped up from lying on her bed, as if she were replying, "Wha'd you say?"

"Wanna go to the park?" I repeated excitedly. As she jumped up, I clicked the unsubscribe link for the email recipient, set my computer on the table, and stood up. Dakota followed me closely through the dining room, where I threw on my jacket, and to the sunroom, where I shoved my feet into my tennis shoes, not bothering to untie them first. Then she led me out the front door.

Our house had blue-gray siding, light reddish-tan brick, and solar panels on the roof. It sat atop a slight hill, among other 1950s houses clad with siding and brick. Our neighborhood was just far enough north from DC to feel suburban, but close enough to access city life, the Metro, good restaurants, and an occasional visit to the Kennedy Center. A middle-class neighborhood, it had a mix of residents: elderly couples and young families, blue- and white-collar professionals, and people of all racial and ethnic backgrounds.

I loved the diversity of Silver Spring compared to nearby towns with reputations for being wealthy and white. I'm white myself but care deeply about racial justice. I began learning about and fighting for racial equity after a police officer killed Mike Brown in Ferguson, Missouri, just north of St. Louis, in 2014. The news hit close to home, literally, because I spent high school, undergrad, and then four years in my late twenties in that area.

In Silver Spring, I volunteered with a local nonprofit, helping to plan two racial equity-based forums for 2018 electoral candidates, and I enjoyed doing my small part to push for equity in our community. Volunteering also enabled me to meet people, make friends, and do something for once that had nothing to do with animals. After three years of putting everything I had into my job in animal advocacy, it had begun to take a toll on me, so I started to seek out hobbies that would take my mind off of it.

As Dakota and I walked through the front yard toward my car, a flock of house sparrows chirped from a tree across the street. They seemed to be insisting that we leave already so they could go back to whatever they had been doing in the holly tree by our bay window, their home base. In the four-inch gap between the window and the roof soffit, they built nests, sang, and pranced around. Brad hated it. He complained that they were probably pooping in there, and he was concerned it would ruin the wood. I should've felt the same way—after all, it was my house too—but I found joy in listening to their songs and their *pitter patters* from our living room. Sidney the cat took my side. He would sit on the windowsill, chattering at the birds, and, I'm sure, trying to figure out how to jump through the glass window to get them.

Other than the flock of birds, the neighborhood was quiet because most people were inside, enjoying the holiday with their families. We got in the car and I cracked Dakota's window and called my mom.

"Hell-ow?" Her loud, wacky voice filled the air in the car.

"Hell-oww?" I echoed. "Who *is* this?" We both giggled.

Since we usually speak on the phone several times a week, we've had many opportunities to share in these goofy phone antics. In fact, the tradition goes back at least as far as 1998, when I lived in Illinois with my family. I remember joking and horsing around with my mom in her home office one evening when she answered an incoming call using a silly voice. I stood next to her, laughing for a few seconds until her face turned serious and she told me sternly to "hold on." I learned after she hung up that the person had been informing her of the unexpected death of my grandma—my dad's mom.

Sixteen years later in Denver, I was laughing with friends at an amusement park when I checked my phone messages and learned that Brad was in the ICU. He had been participating in army exercises in the hot summer sun as part of a training course in Texas and was suffering from hyponatremia, or dangerously low sodium.

Because of incidents like those, I'm very aware that most of the devastating news I receive throughout my life will likely come during times when I'm joking around and being silly. I think many people would describe that as *inopportune*, but I think I prefer being blindsided by bad news to the alternative: living a less joyful life, expecting sadness around every corner. That said, at age thirty-five, I hadn't yet received much bad news, so what did I know.

"Merry Christmas, my daughter," my mom said over the car speakers. "Are we going for a walk?"

"No, we're gonna go to the dog park. I need a little break from work."

"Ohhhh. Is Brad back home yet?" She knew he'd gone back to Illinois to briefly visit his family, even though I couldn't take time off work. In fact, she'd seen him the day before when he'd stopped by her house to say hi and pick up our presents: a brand-new iPad for each of us. Despite my brother and I begging them not to, my parents show their love by giving gifts. I've invited them several times to celebrate the holidays by paying off my mortgage for me, but they don't like that idea.

"No, he's at the airport. He lands at three," I answered. As I drove, Dakota leaned against the locked car door, looking out the window at the passing scenery.

"He'll probably be glad to get home to you and Doggy. And Kitty."

I thought at least a part of her was projecting; *she* would be happy for Brad to be home with me. My mom is proud of my independence, but her top priority is my physical safety, even though I'm a grown woman. She's glad I chase my dreams, but I think she'd prefer me to do so while attached at the hip to Brad, a man who can protect me from danger. When Brad and I were newlyweds, living far away in North Carolina, she'd ask me over the phone if my car doors were locked while I was driving. She'd ask Brad why he "let me" go out at night by myself. Of course, this only made me want to do it more.

If my mom had her way, I would never be alone. Lucky for her, Dakota served as a pretty good protector when Brad was elsewhere. When we lived in Denver, Dakota and I would walk around outside our condo, even along the questionable parts of Colfax Avenue, a main road with a reputation for being dicey. But with Dakota by my side, I never felt unsafe—even after an incident when two strange men followed Brad and me home from a restaurant. I knew Dakota would scare off any creeps. Years earlier, outside our duplex in California, I stood with her in our front yard during a nearly pitch-black night. On the street that intersected our cul-de-sac, a man walked by slowly, looking in our direction. Apparently sensing something she didn't like, Dakota moved to the end of her leash, stood tall, and growled a serious warning at him. The man picked up speed and disappeared down the street. *Good girl, Dakota.*

"Brad will be glad to do nothing for a couple days," I said to my mom, shifting the trajectory of the conversation away from safety and traditional gender roles to fun and relaxation. "He gets tomorrow and the next day off."

"Are you gonna do anything fun?" she asked. We weren't. This was my busiest time at work so I couldn't take time off, especially during the last week of the year.

My mom and I kept chatting as I drove to the dog park. She told me that my brother, Chip, and his wife, Karla, were coming over later and that my dad had picked up pizza and they might play a game.

I didn't miss going home for Christmas, but I did feel left out when my parents got together with Chip and Karla, regardless of whether or not it was for a holiday. They lived close—my parents in a town just east of St. Louis, on the way to Mascoutah, and Chip and Karla thirty minutes west in St. Louis County. I asked my mom if they wanted to FaceTime later, and she said yes. We talked about the weather and how the dogs— Dakota and my mom's little dog, Sophie—were doing. My mom joked that she wanted to mail me a doll for Christmas because she missed me being little. "Don't do it," I warned her.

I steered my car into the parking lot and took a spot near the path to the dog park. "Okay, we're here, so I'm gonna hang up now." I held the key in the ignition, waiting to turn off my car.

"Okay, my daughter. I love you! Merry Christmas."

On the way to the gate, Dakota pulled on the leash a few times, excited to see the other dogs.

"Hold on," I told her.

Once inside the first gate, I unhooked her red leash from her matching collar and opened the second gate. She happily trotted over to the other dogs, and I hung her leash over my shoulders.

"He's sweet. How old?" I turned to see a thin, middle-aged woman sitting on one of the benches. She was looking at me.

"Mine? She's thirteen," I said cheerfully while smiling at Dakota in the distance, hoping to head off any pity the woman might be tempted to show us. That happened sometimes when I told strangers Dakota was in her teens. I hated it. *We're doing great.*

"*She.* Sorry about that."

"Oh, that's okay." I hadn't intended to correct her about Dakota's sex, only to answer her question accurately. But this was a welcomed alternative to discussing Dakota's age.

"She's doing good for thirteen," the woman said.

So much for that. I resisted correcting her again, this time for her grammar. *She's "doing well," I thought. And not "for her age."*

"Yeah, we're going for twenty," I proclaimed.

"Oh, don't we all wish," the woman said with a laugh.

I smiled but slowly walked away from her, trying to signal politely that I had nothing more to say. When I tell people Dakota's age, I almost never enjoy the conversations that follow. They always say the wrong thing to me, for example, that Dakota's doing well for her age or something truly insensitive like "Aww, my last dog lived to be thirteen." These conversations, though usually short-lived, triggered all my complicated feelings about the possibility of losing Dakota one day. I didn't want to have to deal with those thoughts at the park. Being at the park was supposed to be fun. But even in situations more conducive to self-reflection, I didn't like thinking too deeply about it. I had said goodbye to too many dogs throughout my life, and I couldn't bear the thought of ever losing Dakota. Even when she was a puppy, I steered clear of mentioning end of life. So did Brad. One of us would cover her ears with our palms or replace words such as *death* or *dies* with vague descriptions like "far, far in the future, when it comes time." Or we'd skip the word entirely and replace it with a gesture as if to say, "a terrible word goes here." By our midthirties, you'd think we'd have been more mature about it. Especially since, as a physician, Brad had dealt with life and death many times. Nope. We just avoided the subject altogether. That is, unless I was insisting "she's never gonna die." Paper beats rock. Stubbornness beats mortality.

But I'm not naive. I know everybody dies, and I knew that dogs Dakota's size had an average life span of ten to thirteen years. Nevertheless, I wanted to pretend the rules didn't apply to her. I wanted to push the harsh reality of aging aside and ignore it. My love for her left no space for realism in my heart or brain or wherever love and realism are stored. I'm not the doctor, Brad is.

Making her way around the park, Dakota trotted from dog to dog, trying to sniff each one but getting distracted at every new smell that wafted past her nose. I watched with a big grin. Each time a new dog approached the gate to come in, Dakota ran over to greet them. *She's the welcoming committee,* I giggled.

As she squinted in the sunlight, her mouth stretched wide to accommodate her tongue, which hung out the front. She looked like she was smiling. Her once dark eyebrows, faded by then to match the rest of her blonde fur, still held as much expressiveness and personality as the day we met. Her floppy, triangle-shaped ears were the same as always too: brown at the ends with the right one folded over and the left one cocked, exposing some of the hairless pink underside and giving her a look like she was interested in everything in the world.

Dakota greeted all the dogs and sniffed the humans' hands and pockets for evidence of treats. She stopped at my side and watched the other dogs play, then raised her head to look at me. Still smiling, she panted as if to say, "That was really fun!"

"You ready, girl?" I pulled the leash off my shoulders and clasped it to her collar. "Let's go home."

Back at the house, Dakota napped while I showered, ate, and did random chores to kill time until Brad came home. I emptied the dishwasher and picked up the socks and sweatshirt I'd thrown on the floor that morning. I checked in at work and sent thank-you emails to donors. I completed the new patient form that the specialist's office had sent over a few days earlier. I had already sent them the X-ray from Dr. Braff, the one he'd handed me just a week earlier, saying that Dakota's arthritis "actually doesn't look bad," which caused me to do a happy dance in my mind. We were catching it early, which meant the chances were probably greater that a specialist would be able to slow or stop it. I answered questions about Dakota's age, sex, and medical history. I typed "Lab mix?" for her breed. Their guess was as good as mine. I'd been meaning to get one of those doggy DNA kits, just out of curiosity about her breed makeup. But reasoning that it'd be weird to buy myself an expensive present on Christmas Day, I decided to do it later. *I should be thinking about other people, right? Get it together, Lisa.*

Just before five o'clock, I heard Brad's truck pull into the driveway. "Is that Brad? Go get Brad."

Dakota jumped up and paused to listen for him. When his truck lock beeped, she galloped toward the front door and ran down the three wooden steps to greet him on the landing as he came in. I kneeled on the love seat, facing backward and looking over the half wall that separated this part of the living room from the stairs. I was glad to have Brad home and eager to open presents.

"Oh, hi, Peepers!" Brad sang. He got a few pets in before she turned to go back up the stairs. She leaped up to the first one but overshot it on the second. As her back feet slipped down to the landing, her nails scraped against the wood. "Whoooa!" Brad blurted out as he reached for her.

By then, Dakota had already caught herself, bracing her fall with her front feet on the first step. Brad's hands were on her half a second later, preventing any further slippage.

Feeling helpless, I watched from above. Even if I could've gotten to her in time, our landing wasn't big enough for the three of us. I would've just gotten in the way of Brad reaching her. A swirl of thoughts filled my brain, but I couldn't form any of them into words. Dakota had never slipped on the stairs before and I wondered if this was a fluke or a sign of things to come. There was more to it than simply being afraid that

Dakota was getting old. Ever since one of my childhood dogs slipped on a hardwood floor and led my parents to rehome her, Dakota becoming hurt or injured from slipping on hardwood had been one of my greatest worries. If it happened, it wouldn't actually cause much of a problem—we could easily cover the floors with rugs—but the idea of it happening triggered deeply rooted emotions from my past.

Even if I could've articulated my thoughts or emotions, I kept my mouth shut when Dakota slipped. Instead, I let out a long exhale as I walked around the love seat to meet her at the top of the stairs.

"She's okay," Brad said, as if I was blaming him for Dakota's fall. I didn't realize it then, but he was beating himself up inside and compensating for it by acting like it wasn't a big deal. He blames himself for everything, even things he has no control over.

Brad wrapped his arms under Dakota's chest and lifted her onto the main level. I petted her sides with both hands and briefly hugged her around her neck. "You okay?" I asked. "Did you get a little too excited?"

She trotted into the living room, picked up her Kong, and tossed it to Brad. He and I both laughed, relieved by her resilience. "Here," I said to Brad, offering to take the Kong so I could fill it with peanut butter for Dakota. He set it in my palm.

"Hi," he said and gave me a peck on the lips.

After I filled Dakota's Kong with peanut butter, she carried it into the living room and settled in with it. Brad brought his suitcase and backpack inside, setting them in the hallway to deal with later. He told me about the flight and about an annoying guy who gave the airline workers grief in the airport.

I listened as patiently as I could, chiming in with supportive comments, like "Dang" and "That sucks."

When I could no longer keep my cool, I blurted out, "Let's open presents!"

"Okay," Brad chuckled.

A fake Christmas tree decorated with silver tinsel, multicolored lights, and a mix of quirky and classy ornaments stood in the corner of our sunroom. A red Santa hat adorned the top of the tree. Candy canes hung from the higher branches. I knew better than to hang any on the lower branches. Over the past few years, as Dakota's mania for treats had intensified, I'd learned to be more cautious with food. She'd always been food motivated, and, at times, her extreme excitement over treats seemed to prevent her from thinking straight. Brad and I called it "food brain." We'd had a couple of recent instances of trash can diving and counter surfing. Then a few months before Christmas, Brad had come upstairs from the basement to help me with something, leaving a burrito unattended on a plate on the coffee table. Neither of us had noticed Dakota stealthily make her way downstairs. When Brad returned to the basement, the burrito was on the floor with a bite taken out of one end. Next to it was a bit of regurgitated burrito with habanero peppers in it. Dakota had already gone back upstairs, fleeing the scene of the crime.

I sat by the Christmas tree and looked at the dozen wrapped presents. We didn't usually buy gifts for each other, preferring instead to take trips together or go to comedy shows or plays. Plus, I felt weird buying a gift for someone I shared a bank account with, especially because Brad made most of the money that was in ours. It would be like, "Here, you bought this for yourself." That year, though, Brad had bought me presents after I surprised him by decorating the house while he was at work. "You started it," he'd said. "We can't have a tree without presents underneath it."

After Brad bought me a couple of gifts, I bought him a few, and it turned into a competition. We added two gifts for Dakota, as well. I don't appreciate tradition, and I resist any holiday on which you're *supposed* to do certain things (so, basically, any holiday), but I was excited about having a tree and presents that year.

Brad had gotten his mom, stepdad, and sister each a present too. A more traditionally supportive wife might've done that on her husband's behalf—bought the perfect presents with the perfect gift wrap and ribbons on top. But I'm not that kind of wife. Luckily, Brad isn't that kind of husband. He and I agree that it's his job to take the lead with his family, and the same is true for me and mine. He's never wanted a wife who doubles as his mother or his secretary. In fact, that would make him feel infantilized, and he would use that exact word to describe it. He doesn't want me to "take care of him." He can take care of himself. *I* married an *adult*.

Dakota finished her Kong and came to lie beside me. I set one of her presents on the floor in front of her. "Oh my gods!" Brad said, doing her voice. (We'd decided years ago that she was a polytheist.)

"Here! Get it!" I coaxed as I patted the small box with my hand.

Dakota sniffed it and placed one of her front feet on top of it to hold it steady while she ripped off little pieces of wrapping paper with her teeth. I sat in front of her, giggling and recording it with my phone. After a few minutes, I gave her a little help removing the paper, and we revealed a new chew toy—a thick, white piece of hard plastic with a green rubber sleeve wrapped around the middle section. Dakota didn't play with toys anymore, but she still liked to chew on Nylabones. Even so, she set it aside and looked to see if there was any more wrapping paper to rip up.

I directed Dakota to the second gift, which she opened with just as much gusto as the first. Inside was a bag of treats. She sniffed the bag for a second, then looked up at me, hoping there would be a third gift to rip open first.

"That's all we got, puppy. All gone." I showed her my empty hands and she lay down nearby.

Next, it was my turn to open a present. I reached for the box that had been sitting under the tree the longest. Brad had wrapped it in decidedly non-Christmas paper—maybe something left over from a wedding or a birthday. I liked the defiance it showed. *Take that, tradition!* Written on it in black marker was:

Too Lisa
Forum Brad

He'd spelled the words wrong on purpose, thinking it'd be funny to push my buttons. And he was right. Inside the paper were two pairs of socks: one with Dakota's smiling face all over them and one with Sidney's funny face, which was cut out from a photo of him lying upside down.

"These are awesome!" I exclaimed as I held them up in the air. I got Facebook ads for them all the time, and I'd wanted a pair of Dakota socks for a while. Sidney socks were icing on the cake!

Brad opened a fidget spinner that I'd ordered for him after seeing on an episode of *Shark Tank*. "Heh, cool. Thank you!" he said, twirling it in his fingers. Since he'd quit smoking in 2008, his anxiety often showed up as movement, like bouncing his knee up and down as fast as humanly possible. I figured a fidget spinner would come in handy.

Dakota exhaled and flopped onto her side. "Aw, she's bored," Brad said.

I balled up the wrapping paper and tossed it to her, and she held it in place with her paws while she shredded it with her teeth.

As Brad and I opened more gifts, we paused to watch Dakota. We laughed as she tore off small pieces of wrapping paper.

After our gift exchange, we picked up all the scraps. "Good job!" I praised Dakota. "Thank you for my presents," I said to Brad. Then I grabbed my laptop to check in on the fundraising campaign. It would consume my next six days.

In January, things will calm down at work.

In January, Dakota will go see a specialist.

Goodbye #2

Shortly after Lucky died when I was a toddler, my parents got Lady, a beagle. I can only imagine how that conversation went.

"What interests you in getting a dog?"

"Our other one just died from eating poison. Where do we sign to take this new one home?"

Lady was playful and great at hide-and-seek. My mom would hide behind a door or in a closet and Lady would find her using only her nose. Lady's nose, not my mom's. I could make a joke here about my mom having a big nose, but she's a kettle and I'm a pot, so I'll just leave that one alone.

Three or four years after getting Lady, my dad's job transferred him from Texas to Germany. He worked for the US Air Force, and I guess they needed someone in Berlin who could do . . . whatever it was my dad did for work. My parents didn't want to put Lady through the move overseas, so they found a woman who wanted to adopt her, and we said goodbye.

I remember being sad and not understanding what would be so terrible about bringing Lady overseas with us. My parents explained that we'd have to ship her over in the cargo area of a plane, then quarantine her in a facility for two weeks once we arrived. But I wasn't able to comprehend what that would be like for her. Later, as an adult with a dog and cat of my own, I was better able to understand my parents' decision. In fact, it's kind of a running joke in my house that I ruined Brad's dream of ever living overseas because I refuse to put the animals through that.

The woman who adopted Lady gave me her address before we left so I could write to her and check on how Lady was doing, which I did at least once or twice over the next few years. She wrote me back and sent a few photos. I still have them in the plastic tub in my office closet.

Narrowing

I had no idea what to expect walking into the lobby of the specialist's clinic in early January of 2019. Dakota entered first, stretching her neck in an effort to smell every inch of the floor. I stopped at the reception desk just inside the door to my right, and, as I picked up the pen to sign in, Dakota tugged hard in the direction of an Australian shepherd. She wanted to smell and be friends with everyone.

When I tugged on Dakota's leash to gain control of her, I pulled too hard. Her front feet slid on the tile floor, almost causing her legs to splay out. *Shit.* I wrapped the leash around my right hand and held the slack up with my left. She steadied herself and continued pulling toward the shepherd, who watched on calmly from his owner's side. "Don't pull," I said. I was talking to her but I also wanted the people around me to hear it. If they had seen her almost fall, I wanted them to also see that I was a concerned and caring dog owner.

"Dakota, no," Brad scolded. Then he held out his hand toward me and said, "Here, I can take her over to a seat."

Careful not to loosen my grip before he grabbed the leash, I passed it to Brad and watched the two of them walk toward the opposite side of the lobby. As I finished signing us in, I looked around. Instead of chairs, a row of semiprivate booths spanned the length of the rectangular room. Two other people waited in the lobby with their dogs, the Australian shepherd and another whose breed I didn't know—some kind of collie or perhaps a heeler. I worried for a second that we weren't supposed to be there, that maybe this kind of vet's office was meant for working dogs, like bomb sniffers and police dogs. *Oh, who cares*, I told myself. Even if that was the norm, it wouldn't have stopped me from going there. Although Dakota was a nonworking dog, we were willing and able to spend professional level dough on her care.

I wasn't thinking about it at the time, but we'd actually taken Dakota to a specialist before. She'd seen an internal medicine vet in 2013, when she was eight. After witnessing her vomit three times in the span of twenty minutes, I took the morning off work and brought her to her regular vet. After taking an X-ray, the vet reluctantly shared with me that she thought it was either an intestinal blockage or cancer, so she referred us to a specialist for better imaging. During the half-hour drive, Dakota lay on the passenger seat with her ears back, looking uncomfortable and confused. It reminded me of the day I drove her home from the animal shelter when we adopted her. As much as I already loved her back in 2005, it was nothing compared with how I felt about her eight years later. She had become such an integral part of my life and my identity. I glanced at her often on that car ride, scared out of my mind that we might lose her.

The MRI taken at the specialist clinic showed a blockage in eight-year-old Dakota's lower intestine, and she had surgery that same day. Brad and I picked her up the next morning, and, other than an incision in her belly that needed to heal, she was fine. I slept on the couch next to her dog bed for several nights, since she wasn't supposed to use stairs. Once she started feeling more like herself, Brad carried her up to the bedroom every night and back down each morning. I felt lucky that everything went so smoothly.

In the new specialist's office in Maryland, I hoped for a similar outcome. Brad chose a booth on the far side of the lobby, facing a wall with three doors that led to exam rooms. Dakota stood in front of him at the end of her leash, trying to see and smell beyond the privacy of our booth. She had seen the other dogs, but now she could only hear and smell them. No fair.

"C'mere." Brad pulled Dakota over and positioned her on the floor in front of him, between his legs. He gripped her leash and crossed his shins in front of her chest like a safety harness. I sat beside him on the bench.

"Did you get trapped?" I teased Dakota. "That'll happen." With my opposite thumb, I rubbed my hand where the leash had been wrapped.

"That *will* happen," Brad replied in a silly tone.

"Hey, what's that from?" I asked. We'd been saying it for so long that I couldn't remember where we'd picked it up.

"*Super Troopers*," Brad said.

"Oh yeah!"

"We saw it in the theater before anyone else was wise to it. We were ahead of the game." Brad kept watch over Dakota while he reminisced.

She stayed put, but I could tell from her facial expression that her brain was busy. I figured she was hatching a plan: sit still long enough to lull Brad into relaxing his legs, then escape between his knees.

"Look," I said to Brad. "She thinks we were born yesterday."

Brad looked down at her and grinned, amused by her intended deviousness. He kept his legs clenched. Dakota stretched her nose out to get a whiff of the other dogs from inside her leg prison.

I held out my hand for the leash and said, "Here, I'm gonna walk her around."

After Brad handed me the leash, I walked Dakota to our right, past a small kitchen at the far side of the waiting area. I paused to see if she wanted a drink out of the communal water bowl sitting on the floor. She didn't. Instead, she headed into the nook of the kitchenette, where I let her smell around the perimeter of the floor. "No crumbs?" I asked.

Next, I walked her past the other two dogs and their owners, shortening her leash to keep her from invading their space. I thought of Brad as I did this. It was because of his influence that I had any awareness of others' personal space when it came to Dakota. When she'd stolen a toy from a baby on a beach in California back in 2006, I'd laughed at her puppy antics until I realized Brad's embarrassment and remorse. In Dakota's defense, it was a beach where dogs were allowed to run off leash, and I didn't see a single sign about babies being allowed the same freedom. Plus, if the baby didn't want to share the toy, why'd they leave it unattended on a blanket on a beach? Use your head, baby.

If Brad hadn't taught me otherwise, I would've naively assumed that everyone would welcome Dakota's attention. Who wouldn't want to meet and interact with a dog, especially one who was so friendly and good-looking?

Dakota and I completed our lap around the lobby and then I sat back down with Brad. We waited without saying much.

Soon, a vet tech appeared from around the corner. "Dakota?" he asked us.

"Yep," we said in unison.

We stood and followed him to the scale to weigh her. Fifty-three pounds. He noted it on his chart. "Okay, right this way," he said as he led us into an exam room through one of the doors we'd seen. The room was small with a computer desk and a chair for the vet and, across the room, two chairs where Brad and I sat. Between them on the floor lay a thick orthopedic dog bed. *Nice touch, but it's probably lost on Dakota.* She would never lie down at the vet, preferring instead to walk around, smell everything, and stay close to the humans in case one of us was handing out treats.

"So, she's got some arthritis, huh?" the tech asked, looking at his chart while he closed the door.

"Yeah, it's mild, but we want to see if we can slow it down," I said, stroking Dakota's side.

"Everything else going okay? She's eating and drinking fine? No lethargy?" the tech asked.

"Yeah, she's doing great," I added.

The tech asked a few more questions and left us to wait for the orthopedic and sports medicine vet. I tossed Dakota's leash over her back. She had already gotten to work sniffing the floor where other pets had been, being extra thorough at the gaps under the room's two doors. I watched for a moment, happy that Dakota was enjoying herself.

While we waited, Brad texted with his fellow residents at Walter Reed, and I checked my work email on my phone. *Nothing that can't wait till later.* I fidgeted with the PopSocket on the back of my phone, popping it out, then clicking it back in place.

"Man," Brad remarked.

"What?" I asked.

"I'm so glad to be back at Walter Reed. I think I've gotten really set in my ways."

"What do you mean?" I asked.

"Holmes is telling us about the civilian hospital he's rotating at. It's giving me flashbacks. Mario Brothers Syndrome all over the place: the way they do procedures, the nurses, the medical records, everything."

Mario Brothers Syndrome is a term Brad and I use to describe the feeling of frustration you get while watching someone do something differently than you would. We came up with it while playing *Super Mario Bros. 3*, a video game from the nineties. My preferred approach was to secure as many coins, good mushrooms, and stars as possible as I made my way through each level. Brad liked to run as quickly as possible, leaving most of the goodies untouched. When Brad would play, I'd want to yell, "You're missing all the coins!" During my turn, he'd want to ask, "Why are you taking so long?!" And so, the term Mario Brothers Syndrome was born.

"Well, good thing you're in the army then," I joked.

"Shyeah, it is!"

While Brad went back to texting his coworkers, I returned to watching Dakota sniff. She'd gotten dog hair all over the floor, especially by my chair where I'd petted her while talking to the vet tech. *Not quite enough to make a scarf but almost.* Five minutes passed before the vet knocked and entered, smiling. Dakota approached him right away. He kneeled to greet her, stroked her side with one hand, and let her smell the other while he spoke with Brad and me. "We're here about arthritis?"

Brad answered this time. "Yeah, so she's been taking an NSAID for a while, as well as joint supplements—glucosamine and chondroitin. Her arthritis is progressing, and she had two accidents in the house recently, which is completely unlike her. She's 100 percent house-trained. Has been for thirteen years."

Brad glanced at me when he said it. I could tell that he had gotten distracted, if only for half a second, by a feeling of gratitude for what I did with Dakota when she was a puppy. I had trained her. I taught her everything she knew—everything about living with humans, anyway. Brad often thanked me for the great job I did. "She's such a good dog," he'd tell me. It made me feel proud, but I also knew that I had just gotten lucky with Dakota. Sure, I taught her to sit and stay and not poop on the rug, but she's the one who made it fun and easy. She was happy-go-lucky, eager to learn new things, and willing to do absolutely anything that might result in a treat.

In the exam room, the orthopedist looked at Dakota's X-ray on his computer, then did a physical exam. He pushed and pulled on her legs. He watched her move and took note of when she had trouble. He pressed on her back. He bent each of her feet underneath her to see how fast she'd correct them. She put up with all of it without complaint, which was evidence of something else I did right.

When she was a puppy, I'd pet her while she was eating, take her food and give it back, and touch her feet. I didn't do these things to pester her but to get her used to being handled by people so she wouldn't get upset if I needed to take food or toys from her or if a vet needed to do an exam. Recounting that in my head, I felt proud yet again.

I watched this exam the same way I did *any* exam: smitten with Dakota, interested in what the vet was doing with her, but never worried. I had no reason to be worried. In fact, I felt ahead of the curve. Most people don't bring their dog to a specialist to even *treat* arthritis, let alone to ask about preventing it from progressing. Most people would just consider arthritis an inevitable part of the aging process and keep giving pain meds while it got worse and worse.

The orthopedist looked up from Dakota to Brad and me. "I'd like to see if Dr. Anthony, our neurologist, has a moment for a consult," he said with polite professionalism. The word *neurologist* should've given me pause, but it didn't. I already had it in my head that we were there to get ahead of Dakota's arthritis. It didn't even occur to me that she might have a different issue altogether. I'm sure Brad was worried, but I was like, *Sure, bring in more doctors!* I wanted the best care possible for my girl.

After Dr. Anthony came in and introduced himself, the orthopedist showed him Dakota's X-ray and left him to meet with us on his own. Dr. Anthony kneeled by Dakota and did a physical exam that looked a lot like the one the orthopedist had done. This time, I watched more closely, partly curious and partly annoyed that he was just repeating things.

When Dr. Anthony pressed down on Dakota's lower back, she bent her legs, lowering her body to cushion the pressure. I uncrossed my legs and recrossed them with my left leg on top, sliding forward in my seat. "See how she moves to avoid the pressure I'm exerting?" Dr. Anthony asked us.

Yeah, well, stop doing that, I thought to myself.

Dr. Anthony rose from the floor, sat on the stool at the desk, then swiveled it in our direction. Dakota made her way to the comfy bed and lay down, which surprised me.

The neurologist directed our attention to the X-ray on his computer monitor. "Her hips look fine. Great, actually—especially for her age."

There it was again: "for her age." I chose to ignore it and kept listening.

"But if you look over here . . ."

Wait, what's that now?

He pointed to the part of the image at the edge of the film. Dakota's spine. He said it looked like she might have some narrowing in the space between her vertebrae; in other words, the "disk space." They were just two small words, but in that moment, they felt enormous. We came in for advice about Dakota's arthritis—run-of-the-mill, all-dogs-get-it arthritis. I never expected to hear that there was something more serious going on.

Dr. Anthony spoke quickly, or at least it seemed that way. Like how a foreign language sounds faster when it's unfamiliar. Most of the words were common, but he was stringing them together too quickly and interspersing them with terms that belong in textbooks, not conversations. I tried to follow along, attempting to quiet my mind so I could comprehend it. Still, I only caught bits and pieces:

"The symptoms fit a diagnosis of lumbar (something) stenosis."

"Compression at the base of the spine, by the tail."

"Causes incontinence and decreased mobility over time."

"Changes in gait, knuckling."

"Common in shepherds and Labs."

I could feel my face flush. It was a familiar feeling, one that cropped up anytime I felt nervous, embarrassed, or, well, any emotion at all. I took in a long, deep breath and let it out, all the while keeping my lips close together so the vet wouldn't notice. He alternated between looking at Brad and looking at me, and when his eyes were on Brad I took the chance to swallow hard without being seen.

Brad and Dr. Anthony spoke the same language. They both knew the letters and numbers of the vertebrae in Dakota's back. They were nodding. They both seemed calm. *Must be nice.*

I did my best to remain engaged in the conversation while feeling a bit like I do at Brad's work events where everyone's a doctor—they all have a common foundation of medical knowledge from which to launch into specific discussions and shared jokes, while I try not to look bored and think about other things, like how to segue into a conversation about animals or comedy. The difference in this situation at the vet's office was that I desperately wished I was in on the conversation at hand.

Thankfully, when the topic shifted to how to address Dakota's problem, I started to understand more. "I do recommend scheduling an MRI if you're comfortable with that," Dr. Anthony told us. "Imaging is the best way for us to see exactly what's going on, but it's not inexpensive."

"That's okay," I chimed in. "We want to do whatever's best."

"An MRI *will* allow me to confirm my suspicion that it's indeed stenosis and rule out things like an inflammatory infection or a tumor," he continued.

"Great. We'll do that, then," I added. What came across as eagerness was actually masked annoyance. I had already agreed to the MRI, but Dr. Anthony seemed to still be talking to us as if we weren't fully on board with it. I understand that vets need to bring up money. It's a big factor for most people, whether they want it to be or not. But we were lucky enough to afford whatever care Dakota needed, and that's what we were going to give her. I was ready to move on.

"Can you give us an idea at this point of what treatment or management options we'll be looking at?" Brad carried the conversation forward. *Thank you.*

"There are surgical options: laminectomy and diskectomy, depending on what the imaging shows," the vet said.

More words I didn't understand. I lifted my arm to scratch the back of my neck, but then I decided it would give away my discomfort, so I ran my fingers through my hair instead. Brad listened without questions about these surgeries. I had a lot, but I could ask them later.

Brad brought up something about medical options, and the vet described physical therapy and steroid injections. I was a little lost, but Brad seemed satisfied and I trusted his understanding. When we had no further questions, we stood and Dakota followed our lead. The doctor escorted us to the reception desk in the lobby, where he asked the woman behind the counter to print out an estimate for the MRI.

"If you have any other questions, just give us a call," Dr. Anthony said as he shook our hands. "Dakota, we'll see you soon," he added.

We scheduled the MRI, paid our bill, and thanked the woman behind the counter.

As Brad drove home, I checked on Dakota often from the passenger seat. She was fine. I was the one having problems.

"What did he call the thing he thinks she has? Something stenosis?"

"Lumbosacral. It's the term for the location of the narrowing at the base of her tail. I guess dogs have more lumbar segments than humans." He started to ponder aloud the specific differences between the human and canine spinal columns.

I appreciated the answer and Brad's advanced knowledge about the musculoskeletal system, but the last thing I cared about was the labeling of spine segments. As soon as Brad finished his sentence, I asked a follow-up question to bring our focus back to Dakota. "What does stenosis mean?"

"Narrowing," he said.

"Oh." *Duh, Lisa.* I looked out my window and breathed in slowly. I felt overwhelmed by the unexpected news from the vet but I think I also felt numb. Stunned. Dumbfounded. Arthritis sounded manageable to me, but I perceived a spine problem to be much more serious and unfamiliar. I let out a breath and told myself not to worry. "He was saying it's not critical, right?" I asked Brad. "It comes on slowly. Right?"

"Right," Brad answered. "And her symptoms are mild, so he doesn't think she has nerve impingement. That's a really good thing."

I uncrossed my legs, shifting my body to face Brad. "Why were we talking to a neurologist if it's a spine problem?"

"The spinal cord is part of the nervous system," he answered matter-of-factly.

I laughed through my nose at my own ignorance. "I know," I insisted loudly in jest.

Brad explained, "You've got your central nervous system, made up of the brain and spinal cord. Then you've got your peripheral nervous system, which is all the nerves that branch out from the spinal cord."

"Huh." I barely feigned interest.

"You don't care," he said, reminding himself of his tendency to overexplain.

Turning my head and resting it on the side of my seat, I looked at Dakota again. She lay curled in a ball, resting her head by her tail. I lingered for a moment, thinking about the signs I'd failed to recognize: the slipping on floors, the less graceful navigation of stairs.

"She okay?" Brad asked.

"Yeah."

"You okay?"

I swallowed and managed a confident sounding, "Yeah."

In my head I ran through all the times I'd told Dakota to get up on the couch and she hadn't wanted to. I'd never considered that it might've been painful for her. *How oblivious could I be?*

When we got home, I lay on the couch next to Dakota in her dog bed and googled "lumbosacral stenosis" on my laptop. The predictive text helped me spell it right. Pages of results came up, each one requiring a different reading level or veterinary degree to comprehend. I pored over line after line on the websites of various vet clinics, pet insurance companies, and peer-reviewed and not-so-peer-reviewed journals. The words I'd heard at the specialist's clinic were on these websites too and starting to make more sense to me. As I understood it, dogs (and people) have a tunnel in their spines, where nerves travel and connect to different areas of their bodies. Normal wear and tear from aging can cause the space in that tunnel to decrease. Vertebral disks—the little circular pieces of cartilage between the vertebrae of the spine—can dry, rupture, and spill jellylike fluid into the spinal column.

Because the spine touches and interacts with a lot of other parts of the body, spinal stenosis can cause pain, weakness, and numbness, and its impact can be huge. That's probably why Dakota had been diagnosed with arthritis. She was slipping on the hardwood floors, seemed uncomfortable going down the stairs, and was getting out of bed slowly. That's why she had those accidents in the house too. Dogs with lumbosacral stenosis can have problems getting the signal that they need to go to the bathroom. They can also have decreased control over their tails wagging, and it can be painful for them to walk on stairs and slippery surfaces and to jump up on furniture or into cars. Luckily, in most dogs, it's a slow progression, over several years. And there are things that can be done to fix it, such as the interventions Dr. Anthony had mentioned: surgery, steroid injections, and physical therapy.

The website descriptions of the surgery were harder to understand than most of the other parts I read, but they sounded positive, like surgery was a good option for dogs with what Dakota had. It sounded like the best way to go. *Whatever will fix it is the best way to go.*

Solutions and Styrofoam

O ver the next few days, Brad and I made small changes around the house to ensure Dakota's safety in light of her probable spine issue. We blocked off the wooden stairs with a baby gate to keep her on the main level. I bought a bunch of small rugs to cover the slippery floors throughout our house. And we bought a TV.

We already had two, but they were both in the basement— one in our home gym and the other in the family room, where Brad played video games once or twice a week. He, Dakota, and I usually spent a couple of hours in front of that TV in the evenings too, with the humans lounging on the futon and the dog snoozing in her bed. Since Dakota wasn't supposed to use the stairs anymore, we wanted to spend our evenings on the main level instead, so we got a third TV to put in the living room.

I sat on the love seat while Brad unboxed the new TV. As he sliced through the tape and removed the Styrofoam and clear plastic, I asked him about the options that the neurologist had presented to us a few days earlier. We'd be going back to the specialist the next day for Dakota's MRI, and I was determined to be more prepared than last time.

"So the word *medical* just means not surgical?" I asked.

"Yeah," he said, sounding surprised. "Medical treatments are like the steroid injections or pills. Anything that's not surgery."

"Huh." It's amazing how you can use a word so much and think you know what it means before finding out you were wrong. It's like when Brad and I struggled to finish *The New York Times* crossword puzzle one time because the final word was *shinny*, and we thought it was *shimmy*. Apparently, you can also *shinny* up a tree?!

I continued my line of questioning. "So if there's a surgical option, though, why wouldn't we just do that? Like, why would there be any question?"

"Because," Brad said, as if the rest of the answer would be obvious to me. Realizing it wasn't, he added. "Surgery isn't a cure-all. Sometimes it doesn't help, sometimes it makes things worse. And there are always side effects. Like, she could have even more issues *because* of the surgery. She could have a hard time recovering. You don't just get surgery and go back to 100 percent."

I didn't respond. I hadn't expected this. I felt taken aback, defensive. I'd never heard surgery talked about like that. Brad was saying it's not a sure bet. But I thought it was. *Of course, there are always potential risks, but aren't they rare? Don't doctors just tell patients about the risks in order to cover themselves legally?* If there was a surgery that would fix Dakota's spine problem, I wanted us to do it.

"Okay, I'm gonna need your help," Brad said, interrupting my spiraling thoughts. I looked up at him. "Can you hold this box in place while I slide the TV out?" he asked.

"Yep." I bent down in front of the box, stretched out my arms, and gripped each side of it. "Go for it."

Brad lifted the TV then set it on the floor by his feet and steadied it with his hands while he examined it. "Okay, cool." He laid it gently on its side and started attaching the stand to the bottom. I set the empty box aside.

"So the steroid injections are less risky?" I asked, changing the subject from surgery since we weren't getting anywhere with that at the moment.

"Yeah, they just put a needle in the disk space and shoot steroids in there. It's the same thing I do when I give joint injections."

"Oh. Well, that's cool." I knew Brad's work was similar to what the specialist did for dogs, but I hadn't realized just how similar. He talked about steroid injections all the time—so much so that I joked about it being all he did at work. He'd stick needles in people's shoulder joints or spines or knees, and their pain and inflammation would decrease.

"It's kind of a big needle," Brad added, "but she'll be sedated, and they'll give her pain meds."

"Good," I said, not really stopping to think about what he'd just said.

"I'm actually really impressed by the study the vet was talking about," Brad said. "I found it online, and it's legit." He set the TV upright next to his feet again. "Think you can help me lift this onto the entertainment center?"

"Yeah." I placed my left hand under one side of the TV and my right on the edge near the top.

"Careful not to touch the screen," Brad said.

"I know," I snapped back.

"Okay, I was just reminding you. Ready?"

"Yeah."

We lifted the TV and set it gently on the wooden entertainment center Brad had put in the living room earlier that day.

"Nice," I said.

"*Another* color box?" I added, doing Dakota's voice. When she was a puppy, we had decided that she would "say" certain words incorrectly and make up words or phrases for things she didn't know the names of. TV became "color box." *Fireplace* became "scary hole." *Hysterectomy* turned into "histadectomy," an important word for a spayed dog to have in her vocabulary.

Brad turned on the TV with our new remote and figured out how to set up all the apps we used to stream shows and movies. Dakota was in her bed, so I lay down next to her and pet her belly and chest. I still wanted to get her the surgery, but it wasn't just my call. When it came to Dakota and Sidney's care, I did usually have more say, but this was different. While I was in charge of their food, treats, and training, this was a medical decision. It mattered more and the stakes were higher. Brad and I needed to come to a decision we both felt good about. And with his medical knowledge, he should have *at least* as much of a say as me.

Making decisions about someone else's health care is always difficult. There's no clear right answer. It's even harder when it's a joint decision between two people with different perspectives. Before you get married, people tell you to support each other, to never go to bed angry, and to compromise when you disagree. They never tell you that some of life's biggest decisions can't be solved by compromising. You can't have half a kid or move halfway to the place your husband gets a job. And if your dog is diagnosed with lumbosacral stenosis, you can't do half a surgery.

Goodbyes #3 and #4

Alter moving from Texas to Germany as a kid, my family lived in military-owned apartments, which meant we couldn't have pets. But by that age, around seven, I was already someone who needed animals around. So I used my imagination.

A cast of imaginary animals followed me around, my favorite being a German shepherd named Charlie. I imagined him going everywhere with me, never leaving my side.

Three years later, when we were living stateside again, we could finally get a real dog. My parents took us to the animal shelter in Ocean Springs, Mississippi, where we lived. A room full of puppies was Lisa heaven. I was too young then to have my excitement tarnished by the knowledge that those puppies were homeless.

I immediately fell in love with a shepherd mix with a black-and-tan coat and the sweetest face. She had tan fur above her eyes, resembling eyebrows. When a shelter worker opened her cage and let me hold her, I was transfixed—and done looking. I stayed there, snuggling and petting her, ready to take her home as soon as someone said the word.

While I was planning my future with the shepherd mix, Chip and my mom were across the room falling in love with a little black Lab puppy. I know what you're thinking: I was about to get my heart broken. Nope. My parents decided we could take home *both* puppies. We could all have our way! Well, except for my dad, who I'm guessing was on the fence about getting even one puppy.

We brought both dogs home and named them Lady and Lucky. Yes, those were the names of the first two dogs we'd had. What, like your family isn't a little weird?

Lucky #2, the shepherd mix, was mine, and Lady #2, the Lab, was my brother's. I trained Lucky to sit, shake, and do a few other tricks. But neither dog got as much attention as they needed—even from me, the animal lover of the family. They lived in our backyard and weren't allowed inside the house. I think it was because my mom likes things clean, and dogs and their fur aren't exactly conducive to cleanliness. My brother and I visited the dogs a good amount out in the backyard, but that's the trouble with keeping dogs outside: you have to *visit* them.

When I think about the dogs we had as kids, especially this Lady and Lucky, the guilt I feel is overwhelming. I didn't know any better and I didn't make the rules, but I wish I had spent more time with them and lobbied for them to be considered part of the family more than they were. I think it was a different time—that our parents' generation thought differently about pets—but I don't really know. I guess it might've been the place where we lived too. In rural areas, folks often have a different relationship with their pets. It's normal to keep them outside in a backyard or a pen.

I don't think we ever walked Lady and Lucky or took them to dog parks. And I don't have any memories of taking them to the vet, but maybe I'm wrong and we did. We left them in the backyard inside a chain-link fence, while we hung out inside as a family and even when we went on trips to Tennessee and Iowa. We didn't even hire dog sitters; we just left them enough food and hooked their automatic water bowl to the hose.

When we had to move again, the dogs were given away. I was fourteen years old when my dad got stationed at Scott Air Force Base in southwestern Illinois. Before we moved, he went there for a few days to scope things out and look for a house where we could have dogs. Back then, it wasn't as easy as going on Craigslist or Zillow. Not that Craigslist is a walk in the park or anything. Those Missed Connections? Yikes!

My dad wasn't able to find us a rental house with a fenced-in yard and a landlord who would allow our dogs. And I don't think my parents would've entertained letting the dogs live inside at the time. With no other options available, we were put on a waiting list for housing on the air force base, and, in the meantime, we lived for a few months in a very small apartment. No dogs allowed.

So one day, a woman and her young son parked in our driveway. The woman talked to my mom for a few minutes, then opened the door to her back seat and Lucky climbed in. She didn't even hesitate. She did it with so much trust and curiosity. I watched, standing in the grass in the front yard, devastated. I'd spent the last four years bonding with Lucky, and then, without much fuss, she was in some lady's back seat heading out of my life forever.

Was I happy or sad that Lucky didn't hesitate to go off with these strangers? I like to think I was glad, but I honestly don't remember. I can't seem to relive this event without clouding it with my current perspectives, and present-day Lisa is very glad that Lucky went so willingly. I can only imagine how much harder it would've been for my teenage self if Lucky had resisted getting in the car.

In the two days between losing Lucky, and Lady's new family taking her away too, Lady was allowed to sleep in the garage where it was cooler, dry, and partially carpeted. I remember lying with her on that old carpet, crying because I missed Lucky and because I could tell Lady did too. She was always energetic, but as the only dog, she wasn't anymore.

I don't remember anything about Lady's new family. I want to say they drove a truck, but that makes me wonder if they left with her in the truck bed, so I think it's better that I just don't remember.

First Shot

It was seven thirty in the morning and the clinic was calm. Brad leaned to the left to balance his backpack, which weighed down his right shoulder. He grasped Dakota's taut leash in his left hand, while she craned her neck to smell the floor just beyond her reach. A vet tech stood in front of us with a pen and a clipboard in his hands. "What's the best phone number to call you at when she's ready to be picked up?"

"Oh, we'll just wait in the lobby," I clarified. I stood tall, my small backpack perched on my body like a turtle shell and my hair in a ponytail, the ends still wet from my shower. Someone from the clinic had called me the previous morning to confirm our appointment, and I had asked them if we could wait there rather than dropping off Dakota. They said we could, so Brad and I both came prepared to do some work while we waited.

"She might not be finished for several hours," the tech said. "We have to see when we can get her in." He said he'd know more once the vet arrived.

"That's okay. We don't mind waiting." *In other words, we're not leaving, bro.*

I don't know if he wanted us to leave or just wanted to warn us about what we might be in for, but it annoyed me either way. This may have been a routine appointment for the clinic's staff, but it was a big deal to me. My dog was going under anesthesia, and a veterinarian was going to confirm or deny that she had a problem with her spine. We weren't just going to drop her off and go home to work, like this was a typical day. Plus, I didn't want Dakota stuck in a cage after the MRI. Even when we lived in an apartment and I'd take her to the pet store for baths, I'd tell them to give her back to me wet so they wouldn't stick her in a cage to dry.

When the tech relented and walked Dakota into the back area, Brad and I took a seat in one of the semiprivate booths in the lobby, setting our backpacks on the floor in front of us. Moments later, one of the receptionists peeked around the corner and offered, "You can sit in one of our private waiting rooms if you'd prefer. It's a little more comfortable." She had seen us speaking with the tech and probably noticed all our gear.

We jumped at the chance for more space and privacy, so she showed us to the room, which was just across from the reception desk, near the front entrance. She opened the door for us and straightened up the few magazines on the round coffee table in the middle of the room.

"All set," she announced.

"Thank you," I called as she walked out. Four cushy chairs sat around the coffee table. Brad tossed his coat and backpack onto one chair and sat in another. He set his laptop on the table, looked left and right, then pulled the power cord out of a zippered pocket and plugged it into the outlet he'd spotted. I set my coat on top of Brad's and sat in the chair across from him. I slid my laptop out of my backpack and opened it onto my lap. While it booted up, I checked my email on my phone.

"Some of my fellow residents think it's ridiculous that we're spending thousands of dollars on an MRI." Brad leaned forward in his chair, knees apart and forearms resting on his thighs, eager for me to engage.

I looked up. "Why, what'd they say?" I asked defensively.

"I was telling Rhoades I was coming here today, and he just had this look—like he'd never drop MRI money on a dog."

"Well, *he's* ridiculous."

"Yeah he is," Brad agreed.

Around eleven, a tech called us into an exam room, the same one as last time. Dr. Anthony met us inside. "Dakota is doing fine. We've still got her under anesthesia while we chat about next steps." He pulled up the MRI image on the computer screen and invited us to join him in looking at it. He explained the meaning of the various elements, pointing out Dakota's tail to orient us. He showed us a view from her side and a cross section, as if we were looking through her spinal column from her back end. "This imaging confirms our diagnosis of lumbosacral stenosis. As suspected, we don't see nerve root compression, which is very positive."

Brad stretched his neck forward to see better, his eyes following along on the image as Dr. Anthony spoke. I looked at the image and tried to understand, pretending anytime I didn't. I could tell it was a spine, but other than that, it was just a collection of lines and spots ranging from off-white to dark gray. I couldn't help becoming distracted by the name Dakota Rimmert in the bottom left corner. The idea that Dakota had our last name—any last name—was funny and endearing to me.

Brad spoke on our behalf. "So if we opt for the epidural steroid injections, what does that treatment plan look like?"

"We can give her the first injection today, while she's still under anesthesia," the vet said.

"Oh, great," I said, glad to be able to start right away. I still thought surgery was a good idea, but since Brad had seemed so adamantly against it, the injections seemed like the best place to start. Giving her the injections didn't rule out surgery. That option would still be available if, for some reason, the injections didn't work.

"Let's go for it," Brad replied to Dr. Anthony.

"Okay, we'll administer the first injection now and then get her back out to you as soon as we can."

"Thank you," we both said.

A tech showed us back to the lobby, and we took our seats in the private room. I rested my arms on the armrests of my chair and looked toward the window. A set of transparent beige blinds hung in front of it, blurring the details of the parking lot on the other side. But the sun shined through the long vertical slits along the edges. I scooted my butt to the back of the chair, leaned back, and crossed my legs.

It took Dakota longer than expected to come out of the anesthesia, which annoyed Brad, who likes things to go as planned. When a tech walked Dakota into the waiting room, she was groggy, with her ears back, tired, red eyes, and a slow, unsteady walk. A small, square patch of fur had been shaved off her back, and a needle hole in the center of the shaved patch marked where she'd received the injection. Seeing it gave me mixed feelings. It was evidence of our willingness to solve her problem and get her the care she needed regardless of cost or convenience. But it was also evidence that her issue existed in the first place. My perfect dog with the imperfect spine.

The vet briefed us on how the procedure went, ran through a few of the major bullet points in the aftercare instructions, and mentioned that the clinic also offered physical therapy, which would help Dakota keep her muscles strong and maintain her mobility.

"That sounds good," I said to the vet then allowed myself to get distracted, knowing Brad would keep listening intently. I leaned over Dakota, holding her face in my hands and stroking her head and neck. "Are you high, Peepers? You're a good girl," I whispered to her.

Dr. Anthony gave Brad a few papers with aftercare instructions on them, and Brad passed them to me to put in my purse. On our very slow, careful walk to the exit with Dakota, we stopped at the reception desk to pay and to schedule our second injection and first physical therapy appointment.

Recovery

The back seat of my car belonged to Dakota. No humans had ridden in it since my dad handed the car down to me several months prior. It was blanketed with an orange-and-blue seat cover that, according to Brad, made me look like a Miami Dolphins fan. It was either the blue-and-orange or the black-on-black option, and with Dakota's light-colored fur, black was never a smart choice. The seat cover shielded my floorboard and back seat to prevent this car from becoming carpeted in dog hair like my previous one, which had thousands of blonde hairs threaded into the black fabric.

Dakota spent the ride home from the specialist's office lying in the same position that Brad had put her in. No adjusting to get more comfortable. No sniffing at the window. She just lay there, shivering off and on. Naively, I rubbed her side in case she was cold, being sure to keep my hand far from the injection site on her back.

I picked at my nails and watched the traffic around us. Brad was driving less aggressively than usual, probably because he knew I'd want him to with Dakota in this fragile state in our back seat.

When we arrived home, I played doorwoman while Brad carried Dakota into the house. I shut the car door, then ran up the hill to unlock and open the door to our house. Brad was the strong one, able to effortlessly pick her up out of the car and carry her safely across the yard and into the house. That left me without much to do, so in order to feel useful, the best I could do was clear his way. I stood with my back to the storm door and my arm outstretched to hold the wooden door open while Brad walked over the threshold with deliberate, careful steps. He and I both knew that I wasn't just the doorwoman but also the silently judging micromanager, ready to audibly wince if he bumped her head or feet on any doorways. He held Dakota against his chest, with one forearm around her torso and the other under her thighs. Dakota's head hung down and her ears were low at the sides of her head.

Brad stepped up the three stairs and set Dakota on the living room rug. Before standing back up, he hovered low to make sure she had her balance. Her head and neck swayed as she looked around the room, and her back feet shuffled underneath to keep her steady.

I slid her bed near the couch and stood next to it. "C'mere, puppy. Come lay down," I said as I pointed at the bed.

She just stood in place, staring at me, as her back legs started to bend underneath her.

Crouching near the bed, I patted it with my hand. "Dakota, come lay down," I repeated in a louder voice and deeper tone.

She looked away from me and started to pivot on her bent legs. Brad lurched toward her with his arm outstretched, ready to catch her if she started to fall. She leaned into his steady hand and walked into the kitchen while Brad said with a laugh, "She's so out of it."

"Where ya goin'?" I called.

Brad followed Dakota, and I went through the dining room to meet them. Dakota didn't seem to have a plan; she just meandered through the kitchen and into the sunroom, stopping every few steps.

"What are you doing, Peepers?" I asked. She took another step without looking at me. "Do you need to pee? Maybe she needs to pee."

"Maybe," Brad said, sounding skeptical.

"Will you help me take her out, just in case?"

Brad gently lifted her again and carried her out back and down the steps, setting her in the grass. I stood in front of her. "Go pee, pup." She showed no interest in peeing or being outside or being anywhere. She just stood, holding her head down and looking out through the tops of her eyes.

"She's not gonna go," I told Brad.

"Yeah. We tried."

"Let's bring her inside," I suggested. "Maybe she'll lay down."

Brad carried Dakota through the door, and I closed it behind us. I walked along with Dakota, straddling her torso and gently aiming her toward the living room. I couldn't get her to go straight through the dining room, so we roamed through the kitchen instead. Once in the living room, I steered her toward her bed, but she just stood in front of it. She seemed determined not to cooperate, unsatisfied with every available option.

"C'mon, puppy. Lay down." I sat on the couch and dangled my hand over her bed. "Dakota, lay down, please," I begged. I hated seeing her uncomfortable, and I was starting to feel frustrated. I didn't know how she was feeling, but I imagined it as a mixture of confusion and physical pain, neither of which she nor I could do anything about. She was already on the post-procedure pain medicine the vet had given her, and only time would lessen the effects of the anesthesia.

She ignored me, instead turning around again and heading toward the dining room. "No, Dakota. C'mon. We're not going in there." I straddled her body and put my hand on her chest to keep her from moving forward. "Should we block her off in here?" I asked Brad, looking up at him from my bent-over position above Dakota's frail, unsteady body.

"Maybe," Brad said, which was code for: "Sure, but I don't know if it's gonna help." He moved her food and water bowl into the living room, and I brought in a chair from the dining room table and leaned the edge of the baby gate against it to block the wide space that led from the living room to the front steps, hallway, and kitchen doorway. Brad set up two chairs in the entryway to the dining room.

After another winding loop around the living room, Dakota lay down in her bed. I raised my arms over my head, pumped my fists in the air, and mouthed the word *yes* to Brad. But before I could even put my hands down, Dakota was getting out of bed. She stumbled across the room, her legs buckling beneath her as she walked. It seemed futile to try convincing her to lie down, so I followed her lead instead, standing by to grab her if she teetered. She stumbled to the baby gate and turned around. I caught her when she almost fell. Then she stumbled to the chairs blocking the dining room. This time, she turned around more successfully. Finally, she returned to her bed—not in it, but next to it. She stood. We watched.

"Eh?" Brad tilted his head and raised his eyebrows in anticipation.

"Eh . . . I'm not holding my breath," I said with more than a hint of doubt. I watched skeptically as Dakota climbed into her bed, first one front foot, then two.

"Ope!" I whisper yelled, hopeful that she'd lie down but not wanting to interrupt her process.

She placed her back feet into the bed and lay down with her front paws on the edge. She didn't look comfortable, but if she could lie down, maybe she could fall asleep and snooze off the pain and confusion. And at least she wouldn't be walking around, risking a fall. I sat on the couch, watching her for a few minutes. Brad and I smiled at each other when Dakota lowered her head onto her paws. When she shivered, I covered her with a blanket, hoping she was cold and not in pain.

It took a few minutes, but Dakota stopped shaking and fell asleep. I stayed nearby, watching TV from the couch and keeping an eye on her. Brad headed to the kitchen to make some lunch. Sidney, who had been keeping his distance so far, snuck over to smell Dakota. Seeing that she was asleep in her bed, he decided to take advantage of her altered state. He loved snuggling with her, and it worked best when she was unconscious. Otherwise, his incessant kneading and licking tended to get him kicked out of the bed. He curled up against Dakota's belly, tucked his head down, and fell asleep.

When Dakota woke up to readjust her position, Sidney jumped out of the bed. He scares easy. Dakota's blanket fell off, exposing the patch of bare skin on her back. I stroked the side of it with my index finger, careful to avoid the injection site.

Dakota slept off the anesthesia, and by the next day, she was alert, walking fine, and asking to go outside to sniff for forbidden treats that wild animals likely had left in our backyard. She was back to her old self. *One injection down. Two to go.*

Ramping Up

C ome see."

"Huh?" I wiped the corner of my eye and squinted. It was a Saturday, a couple of weeks since Dakota's first injection.

Brad stood at the side of the couch, smiling. "Come see the ramp!" he exclaimed.

I pressed the button on my phone and saw that a few hours had passed since he'd gone outside to work and I'd lain down for a nap. I tossed off the blanket and sat up.

"Dakota, c'mere!" Brad said, flapping his arms at his sides like a penguin, signaling to me his excitement for her to see the ramps he'd just built.

Her ears perked up and she looked at Brad with curiosity. When I stood up, she did too, and we all walked over to the sunroom. I grabbed my jacket off the back of a chair as I cut through the dining room, then I slipped my feet into Brad's old Vans. After Brad opened the door for Dakota and me, she walked through and I shuffled along behind her in shoes six sizes too big.

The first ramp laid atop the three stairs that led from our back door to our deck, leaving about sixteen inches of each step exposed on the right side. The ramp was about six feet long and covered in black rubber. White wooden trim lined the sides and a few strips were placed horizontally across the top of the ramp. If Dakota somehow slipped on the nonslip rubber covering, the wood trim would keep her from sliding very far.

A second, nearly identical ramp sat securely at the edge of our deck, where a single step led into the yard. The quality of the ramps impressed me; they looked almost professionally done. When Brad told me he was planning to build them, I knew he'd do a good job, but I didn't know they would look *that* good.

Brad and I both watched to see what Dakota would do. He stood in the middle of the deck, near the bottom of the first ramp, while I stood behind her at the top. She sniffed the black rubber, held up her head, and then trotted down the stairs, sidestepping the ramp.

I burst out laughing.

"She hates it!" Brad whined, feigning self-pity.

"No, she doesn't! She just needs to get used to it," I reassured him.

Dakota walked around the deck, smelling the construction supplies that littered our backyard: wood scraps, paint cans, and strips of black rubber flooring. Brad had purchased all the items that morning at the hardware store. He'd also bought a table saw. Usually, the purchase of a large, expensive tool for a one-time project would bother me, but it was for ramps to make Dakota's life easier, so how could I be upset about that?

Dakota stepped down from the deck to the grass, completely bypassing the second ramp. She sniffed around, peed, then hopped up the step.

"Ridiculous," Brad said, shaking his head at her.

"It's muscle memory," I told him. "She's gonna need to use them a bunch of times before it becomes habit."

"Yeah, yeah, yeah," Brad grumbled as he started to clean up the tools and supplies from our patio table. He shoved the strips of rubber into our brown trash can, then added two poop bags I had tossed beside it after walks. *Dang it*, I scolded myself silently. *I always forget to pick those up.*

I turned back to watch Dakota. As she headed toward the back door to go inside, I ran in front of her, stood on the stairs to block them, and pointed to the ramp. "Look. Come over here," I encouraged her.

She adjusted her route to follow my gesture, then walked up the ramp without hesitation.

"There we go!" I celebrated.

"Yay!" Brad joined in.

I motioned to the ramp again, this time asking Dakota to walk back down it. When she put her front feet on it, I ran over to the middle of the deck to take a picture of her using it, proud that our backyard was officially senior-dog friendly, although, at the time, I called it "wheelchair accessible" because I still couldn't quite admit that Dakota was a senior dog.

Later that day, I posted a picture on social media of Dakota on her new ramp. I gave Brad a shout-out in the caption:

Dakota loves her new ramp made by Brad Rimmert!!!

When I think back to all the times I've been most grateful to have Brad as my life partner, the day he built Dakota the ramps is in my top ten. At that point, Dakota wasn't supposed to climb stairs anymore, but our backyard—our sanctuary—had unavoidable steps. She could still take them just fine, but we had no idea how long that would last. We knew there might come a day when she'd find walking up and down stairs too painful, or she might lose all strength in her back legs and need to get around in a doggy wheelchair.

Brad took what could've been a really complicated dilemma and made it easy. Thinking, *I'll just build a couple of ramps*, he did some research, went to the hardware store, and came home with the right materials. Then he spent a chilly winter day measuring, painting, cutting, and hammering, and the problem was solved. Because of him, our backyard would be Dakota-friendly, no matter what the future had in store.

In the Way

When I brought Dakota to her first physical therapy appointment in February, I let her pee in the grass and then paused in front of the clinic to take our picture in the dark reflection of the full-length window. I was excited to be bringing her there, glad that she was on a path to wellness. Plus, I wanted to see her on the underwater treadmill. I'd watched videos online of dogs experiencing it for the first time, and they were inspirational, empowering, and adorable.

After I signed in, Dakota and I waited in one of the semiprivate booths in the lobby. With the leash in my left hand, I held my phone in my right and pulled up the messaging app we used at work. I clicked on Mike's name and hurriedly typed a message to remind him I'd be away from my computer for an hour or two. I felt grateful for the flexibility my job provided, but it was a double-edged sword. I allowed myself to take long breaks during the workday and then felt like I had to make up for them by working in the evenings, unintentionally overwhelming myself.

As I slid my phone into my purse, a tech greeted us for our appointment. "How's she doing? How's her mobility at this point?"

"She's pretty good," I answered. "We're taking really short walks a couple times a day, just around our block."

"Have you noticed any improvement since the first injection?" she asked.

"No, I don't think so."

"Okay. That's alright, it's only been a few weeks," the tech said in a comforting tone. Then she asked for Dakota's leash and I handed it to her, expecting her to invite me to follow them. But she turned around and walked away. With my dog. Through the door. Without inviting me. I thought about stopping her and asking if I could come. But if she had wanted me to come, she would've invited me.

Other people I know have gotten to watch their dogs, but maybe this clinic has stricter rules. Maybe they're all business. That's good, I guess. But I felt like I was missing out. I waited in the lobby, scrolling on social media and checking work messages. I wondered what they were doing and how Dakota had reacted to the treadmill, the water, the moving floor.

After about thirty minutes, the tech approached my booth with Dakota. "She did great!"

Taking the leash, I jostled Dakota's side, which was damp from the underwater treadmill. "Good girl!" I praised.

The second time we went in for physical therapy, I wasn't going to get left in the lobby again. I invited *myself* back. Two treadmills, each surrounded by clear, hard plastic walls about four feet high, stood next to each other. With treats in her hand, one of the two technicians coaxed Dakota into the treadmill tank on the right. Then she closed the tank door and pressed a button to start filling it with water. It must've been warm because Dakota didn't flinch or try to look for an exit. She stayed calm, focusing on the treats. Once the water rose high enough to cover Dakota's chest, the tech pressed the button again to stop the water. When she pressed a different button, the treadmill turned on. It buzzed softly, moving at what looked like one mile per hour. Dakota hesitated a bit but quickly got the hang of it. One foot in front of the other, and you get treats.

For most of the time Dakota was on the treadmill, she kept her front feet planted on the part that was stationary, moving only her back legs. "She's cheating," I joked.

"When you're fourteen, you're allowed to cheat," the tech responded.

I giggled instead of correcting her. *She isn't quite fourteen.*

I was glad to get to see how the treadmill worked. The techs were kind to Dakota, cheering her on and giving her treats. But I couldn't help feeling like I was in the way. The techs were buzzing around the room—the two with Dakota and two others with a second dog who had come in after us. I kept having to shift back or to the side to avoid run-ins with them in the small room. I refrained from taking a video and instead stood in the corner so the techs could do their work.

After a few minutes on the treadmill, one tech gently dried Dakota's legs and torso with a towel and walked us across the hall to a regular exam room for the cold laser therapy. I recognized the comfy dog bed from our first visit to the clinic, but this was a different room, so I guess they had a bed in each one.

I sat in a chair by the door and, again, tried to stay out of the way.

For this part of the appointment, the tech ran a laser over Dakota's legs and back. Supposedly, cold laser therapy promotes healing and helps with pain relief. People say it causes physiological changes to the cells. *Sure, if you say so.* Some people might be surprised to find out that I don't believe in alternative medicine. After all, I'm liberal. I'm a vegan. I'm open-minded about a lot of things. But I just can't wrap my mind around the idea that a *laser* can fix an aging spine.

I hoped I was wrong, though, and that the cold laser therapy would help Dakota. I would've done anything to make her feel better as long as there was no risk to her health or safety.

The laser therapy was supposed to be the easy part of Dakota's appointment. Her job was simply to lie down on the bed and stay still. Now, before we admonish her for not excelling at this, let's take a moment to remember how well she did on the treadmill. Cheating aside, she really nailed it. Besides, her failure to stay still here was the vet tech's fault, not Dakota's. When we first entered the exam room, the tech gave me a treat to give to Dakota, not realizing what a grave mistake she was making. Dakota kept wanting to get up and come over to see if I had any more treats.

It took two nice techs to sit with her and keep her still. They were gentle and kind, of course, but I'm sure it was a little frustrating. I wondered if I should leave the room, but I didn't ask.

On our next visit and every visit after that, I waited in the lobby and let the vet techs do their thing.

Goodbye #5

Once my family settled into housing at Scott Air Force Base in Illinois, after moving there from Mississippi when I was fourteen, we got our third Lady. No, I'm not kidding. She was a black Lab mix, like Lady #2.

I don't remember why, but my parents let this Lady #3 live inside the house with us. Maybe their desire to have a dog began to outweigh their desire for fur-free floors. Or maybe it was my desire. Either way, I'm sure Lady got hair on everything and my mom hated it.

About a year after we adopted Lady, she slipped on our hardwood floor while playing and had to have surgery. For weeks, she wore a splint that covered her entire back left leg.

Once she healed, my parents decided she'd be better off with a family who had more space for her to run around.

I don't remember saying goodbye, so I must've blocked that memory from my consciousness.

Lightweight

I sat facing my laptop on the round table in front of me and watched Brad out of the corner of my eye. He bounced his knee up and down and cracked his knuckles one by one. This went beyond his usual impatience. Dakota had just gotten her second steroid injection, and Brad and I were back in the private room at the specialist's office. "They were supposed to bring her out in ten or fifteen minutes," Brad said, looking at his watch. "It's been almost thirty."

"It took her longer than they thought it would last time too, right?" I said, more as reassurance than an actual question. Dakota apparently had a low tolerance for drugs. We'd even had to decrease the dosage of her pain pills after realizing they made her drowsy. "She's a total lightweight," I added, half joking.

"I'm gonna ask for an update." Brad left the room before I could try to talk him out of it. He knew I thought he was overreacting. He probably thought I was being too passive. He's quick to jump to negative conclusions, and he sees the world as a dangerous place that he must defend himself from. And it often has been. His mom raised him by herself after his dad left when Brad was six. They didn't have a lot of money, and Brad's sister, Dee, has special needs. He often had to fend for himself—making his own dinners at times, earning his own money, and even defending family members against people mistreating them. As an adult, Brad joined the military and fought in the War on Terror in Qatar and Iraq. It's no wonder he thinks I go through life wearing rose-colored glasses.

I grew up with two loving parents, financial security, and more than my fair share of privilege. So, naturally, I see the good in people, and I view new situations as opportunities. I have decades of evidence that things will work out fine for me. And any evidence to the contrary gets ignored or justified by my subconscious mind because it doesn't align with my rosy worldview.

"She's taking longer than they expected to come off the anesthesia," Brad said as he came back in the room. That wasn't new information, of course. It just confirmed what we already knew. He closed the door behind him and sat down. Then he adjusted his watch, picked up his phone, and tried to read something on the screen. When he changed his mind, he set the phone upside down on his leg, gripped it in place with his hand, and bounced his knee up and down.

"You should've brought your fidget spinner," I joked in an attempt to lighten the mood. He purposely ignored my silly facial expression, so I went back to working on my laptop. The next monthly newsletter needed to go out the next day. After realizing there was an error somewhere that would need to be fixed with HTML coding, I gave up and my mind wandered back to Brad. I wished I could do or say something to make him feel less worried. I wished I could transfer some of my optimism to him.

Sitting there, I remembered asking one of Dakota's previous vets about anesthesia risks. When Dakota was ten, while she and I were visiting my parents in Illinois, I noticed her licking at her paw. She had a sore that appeared to have ruptured. I made her an appointment with a vet in the neighboring town, thinking they'd give me some ointment and send us on our way. Instead, they told us Dakota would need surgery. They said it was just a cyst, but because of its location between the pads of her foot, it would just keep rupturing and never heal, so they needed to remove it. They were able to get her in the following morning, but the drop-off time conflicted with a work meeting I'd scheduled with a local donor.

"I can take her," my mom offered.

"In your car?" I asked.

"Yeah," she said.

It's not at all unlike my mom to do something thoughtful for one of her kids, but it was very much unlike her to offer to put a hairy dog in her car. I was amazed. My mom had a nice car and, like everything she's in charge of, it was immaculate.

"Are you sure?" I asked.

She was.

Later, when my dad came upstairs to eat dinner with us, my mom told him the plan.

"In *your* car?" he asked her. She looked at me and rolled her eyes. I laughed.

The next morning, I got up early to go to my meeting. I held Dakota's face in my hands and kissed her head.

"Thank you," I said to my mom and hugged her.

I wasn't there to see the preparations before their trip, but I imagine my mom did a very thorough job of placing a sheet in her back seat for Dakota. I imagine she or my dad took Dakota out on a leash to pee. And I imagine that, when my mom opened the car door, Dakota jumped in, messed up the neatly straightened sheet, and shook fur everywhere. I imagine my mom being frustrated but not surprised, bothered but also amused. I imagine that right when she got home, my mom got out the vacuum and cleaned the dog hair from her car.

That afternoon, my mom and I went together in my car to pick up Dakota, since my car was already very hairy. When I tried to pay the man at the counter, he said it was already taken care of and glanced up at my mom. I turned around to look at her and she was smiling. I don't know how much money it was, but it couldn't have been cheap. After all, it was surgery. As grateful as I was for the financial support, I was even more grateful to my mom for taking Dakota to the appointment. She might think paying for it was the bigger gIft, but offering to take care of Dakota, to let her shed in my mom's car—that was the gift I'll remember. It's one of the best gifts I've ever received.

When Dakota had the cyst removed, the vet who performed the surgery told me that anesthesia isn't necessarily more dangerous for older dogs—that that's only true if they have a heart or respiratory problem. Dakota didn't, so the vet said she'd be fine. And she was.

Still, at the specialist's clinic in Maryland it was taking her much longer than expected to come out of sedation. Brad checked his watch again, then sighed heavily.

"How much time now?" I asked.

"Forty-six minutes." He was officially freaking out. His knee bounced at a speed that looked unnatural and tiring.

"Should we ask for another update?" I suggested halfheartedly, hoping he wouldn't say yes. I wanted his worry to be alleviated, but I also didn't want to annoy the staff or the vet.

"I mean, this is getting ridiculous," Brad responded, saying what he was thinking rather than answering my question.

"I really don't think you need to be nervous."

Just as I finished my sentence, the door opened and Dakota walked in, followed by the vet and a tech.

"There she is," Brad said with relief as he stood up.

I stood too and walked over to Dakota, taking her leash from the vet tech. "Hiii, Peepers."

She looked at me with wide eyes and pinned-back ears. I leaned over, took her face in my hands, and rubbed her neck. She was fine. Groggy, but healthy and awake and fine.

On the ride home, Brad drove and I sat in the passenger seat, turning around often to check on Dakota. She lay in the back seat, shaking off and on. But she was okay. Brad was the one with issues this time around.

"I dunno, man." Brad kept his eyes on the road.

"What?" I asked.

"I dunno if we should do another one of these injections."

What?! We need to finish what we started! I thought to myself. *We only have one more steroid injection left.* I didn't want to talk about it right then. I just wanted to get Dakota home and settled. I stared out the windshield and tried to decide what to say when I could've just said what I was thinking.

Brad sensed my mood. "We can talk about it later."

Caretaking

Around this time, I started to accept that Dakota was old. We had ramps for her at our house, she had a specialist, and she was doing physical therapy and steroid injections. I guess that was finally enough evidence to break me out of my denial. I even went beyond accepting it to embracing it. I began proudly identifying Dakota as a senior dog and myself as a senior dog owner.

I joined a Facebook group called the Senior Dog Care Club, in which members would ask questions and share information about various aspects of caring for elderly dogs. I labeled my Instagram posts with "#seniordog."

I hated that Dakota was aging, but I also loved taking care of her. That surprised me. In no way had I ever thought of myself as nurturing, but I started to. My willingness to put her first also surprised me. Not that I *could* do it but that I *wanted* to. I'd never had the desire to be anyone's caretaker. I value independence, good boundaries, and asking for what you need. I warn visitors to my house that, if they want anything, they need to let me know because I won't keep asking. I joke with my mom that when she gets old, she'll be well taken care of—by my brother and his wife.

I never wanted kids because it sounded unappealing to me to have to shape my life around someone else—to have someone be completely dependent on me.

Our society still views caretaking as the responsibility of women. It's undervalued and it's used to keep women small. The stereotype that women are nurturing has resulted in way too many moms who are martyrs—who feel like they have to put everyone else first and ignore their own dreams and goals. At the same time, the trope of the nagging wife or mother tells women that they care *too* much—that they're high maintenance and unreasonable. If they don't worry, they're bad moms. If they do worry, they need to chill out. It's a catch-22.

However, there's one form of caretaking that's safe from these impossible standards—one that actually makes women *cool*. And that's taking care of a dog. (More specifically, a dog who is at least thirty pounds. A so-called real dog.)

For some reason, dogs (real dogs) are associated with men and boys, and cats are associated with girls. We see this everywhere. Dogs are "man's best friend." They go hunting together, take down criminals, and do other macho stuff we see in movies and on TV. Almost every time a stranger first met Dakota, they referred to her as "he." Guess what gender they assumed Sidney was.

When Chip and I were too young to read, my mom used drawings to help us identify our Christmas presents. She labeled each of Chip's presents with a drawing of a dog, while mine had a cat. It wasn't because Chip had an affinity for dogs.

In fact, if one of us was the dog person, it was absolutely me. I liked cats too, but dogs were my favorite by far. Even though it wasn't purposeful, the message was clear: dogs are for boys, and cats are for girls.

Dogs are man's best friend, and cats are conniving and finicky and high maintenance, just like women.

Because Dakota was a big, adventurous, noncuddly dog, I was allowed to be loving and nurturing with her without being teased or made to feel small. It wasn't associated with femininity. I think that's why, deep down, my friendship with her served as my main outlet for connection and caring, for being mushy and lovey-dovey. Or, who knows, maybe I just don't like kids.

Balance

The week after Dakota's second injection, I almost cried in front of three of my coworkers. But not about Dakota, about Excel spreadsheets.

I sat at the dining room table in the sweatpants and T-shirt I'd worn to bed the night before and a hoodie thrown on top of that. I also wore my rectangular brown frames, not because they helped me see better but because I liked to wear them occasionally for fashion.

Brad and I hadn't yet circled back to our discussion about Dakota not getting a third injection, and that was okay with me. Sometimes, when we realize we're not on the same page about an issue, things just have a way of working themselves out organically. We think through each other's perspectives, and one of us will come back to the other, saying, "I think you were right." I hoped that would happen in this case. Obviously, I wanted Brad to tell *me* I was right.

To my left, Dakota lay curled up in her bed in the entryway between the dining room and sunroom. Aside from the shaved patch of fur with a dot in the middle, she was back to her normal self after her latest steroid injection. I opened the agenda for my upcoming meeting and noticed that Mike had added a main topic to the document:

Increasing monthly donations

Upon seeing it, I moved my hands from my keyboard to my temples. I scratched my head and sucked in air through pursed lips. Blowing it out, I adjusted my glasses and looked at Dakota. "It's gonna be a fun one," I told her. She opened her eyes to see that nothing interesting was going on, then closed them. I minimized the document and resumed working through my emails, trying not to spiral, but failing.

I wasn't very good at being managed. I felt I deserved complete ownership over my tasks and department, so I resented what I knew was coming: Mike would bring to the meeting a plan he'd cooked up on his own, and I'd be asked to merely carry out his vision. But I desperately wanted to be responsible for not only doing the work required to increase our donations but to develop the strategy too. I had the knowledge; I just never felt like I had the time.

I also knew that whatever plan Mike came up with would inevitably lead to me getting in over my head with spreadsheets and formulas—the part of my job I *didn't* think I could do well. I'd procrastinate starting these tasks until I couldn't put them off anymore and then I'd pore over articles on the Internet, take free or cheap online courses, or force myself to call on friends or relatives for last-minute tutorials, thereby admitting I couldn't handle it on my own. Just thinking about it had me tightening my shoulders, clenching my teeth, and feeling panicked.

As I watched the time on my computer turn from 2:59 p.m. to 3:00, I took a deep breath and clicked the meeting link. Soon after, I heard the all too cheerful *bonk* that indicated I had joined, then the faces of my boss and two coworkers appeared on my screen.

After a few pleasantries, Mike brought up the main agenda item. "I think we should send an email series to people who give between, say, fifty and five hundred dollars a year but aren't yet monthly donors."

There it was, I thought. *A preconceived plan that isn't mine. Why do I even* work *here?* Feeling my face and neck flush, I turned off my camera.

My two colleagues chimed in. "That's a great idea!" one of them said.

"Yes, I like that," added the other.

"Lisa, what do you think?" Mike asked. From the black boxes on their computer screens, everyone heard my response. It was one of surrender. "Sure, that sounds good."

When the meeting ended, I closed my laptop, stood up, and turned my soda can upside down above my lips and shook out the last drops. Then I tossed the can into one of our three blue plastic recycle bins in the sunroom. Dakota watched me from her bed. When I slipped my foot into my nearby tennis shoe, she scrambled to her feet.

After switching out my glasses for sunglasses, I grabbed her leash from its spot near the front door, and Dakota began shuffling her feet at my side. "Do you wanna go for a walk?" I asked her. She pranced and whimpered. "Okay. Let's go."

We left out the back door, using the ramp. A long, hilly road called Loxford Terrace encircled our section of the neighborhood. We used to walk all the way around it in twenty-five minutes, including stops for peeing, pooping, and sniffing. Dakota's, that is. I did most of those things at home. Although, to be fair, Dakota still pooped inside the house occasionally too.

This time, we walked around the shorter block: down the hill of our street, then back up Loxford behind our house. Dakota kept her nose to the ground except to glance occasionally at where we were. I kept my eyes lowered too, scanning the ground in front of her for anything that looked like chicken wing bones, dropped cracker crumbs, or gum. If I didn't see it first, she'd gobble it up in what always felt like a fraction of a second.

I kept an eye on Dakota's legs too. By this point in time, her back left foot grazed the sidewalk on most steps. It didn't seem to cause her any concern, so I tried not to let it bother me either. Even so, I couldn't help but wince each time her nails made a scraping sound against the concrete. The missteps were what really scared me, though. I stood at the ready in case she stumbled over uneven pavement or tree roots sticking out of the ground. I surveyed the area, gripped the leash, and pulled in the slack so I could use her leash and harness to stabilize her and prevent any falls.

We strolled along, me balancing my walking duties and Dakota just balancing. It felt good to get some fresh air.

When I sat back down in front of my computer after our walk, I saw that Mike had assigned me a task:

Pull a list of people who donated between $50 and $500 in 2018 but who aren't yet monthly donors

I felt my face turn red in an instant. The arches fell out of my eyebrows as I pressed my lips together, wrinkling my chin. I thought about the complicated steps a task like this would entail—the queries, the spreadsheets, the data sorting, the stress. I crossed my arms on the table and lay my head on the sleeves of my hoodie. I sat like that for several seconds, dreading every step of this new project. I was already familiar with the shame I knew would come from spending hours on it and then having to admit to someone that I couldn't figure it out.

I lifted my head and clicked to close out of our project management system. "That seems like a good problem for *tomorrow*," I said sarcastically. Then to Dakota, I said, "You wanna treat?" She and I rounded the corner into the kitchen, where I got her a chew and myself a handful of chips.

After studying in the basement that evening, Brad came upstairs, where I was half sitting, half lying on the love seat. My laptop rested on my thighs, and my fingers were dancing on the keyboard.

Brad sat on the couch. "Are you working?"

"Um, yeah, kind of." I honestly wasn't sure. I had work stuff pulled up, but I was also chatting online with a friend.

"Do you have a minute?" He seemed serious.

"Sure." I set my laptop on the coffee table.

"I don't know if we should keep giving Dakota the steroid injections." He was continuing the conversation I hadn't wanted to have the previous week and still didn't.

I felt defensiveness fill my brain, but I stayed quiet.

He must've noticed because he softened his approach. "Or maybe we can ask the vet how much improvement the studies show after two injections."

"Why?" I asked. I started taking deep breaths to keep from crying. The stress from my job and from the steroids not working was a lot to handle, even though I didn't have the insight to understand that at the time.

"She doesn't do well with the anesthesia," Brad continued. "I don't like how long it took for her to fully wake up from it. And the shots don't even seem to be doing anything for her."

"There isn't anything wrong, though. She's just a lightweight, right?" I looked at Dakota in her bed.

"Yeah, Brad. I'm just a lightweight," I said in her voice to ease the tension.

Brad chuckled to appease me. "I mean, it'd be different if we were seeing some improvement."

"I guess so." I rubbed my thumb across the jagged tip of my fingernail. "They keep asking me at physical therapy if I've noticed any improvement, and I say no."

"If anything, her issues are progressing," Brad added.

I had to agree with him about that; so far, the steroid injections weren't working. We had done two, we'd been to physical therapy a few times, and Dakota was still taking carprofen and gabapentin, the extra pain pill, every day. With all that, her mobility should have been improving, but it seemed like it was only getting worse. Brad had lost faith in the possibility that the Injections would help Dakota. I was starting to as well, but I held on for dear life to my last thread of hope. We had one injection left, so, in my mind, we didn't need to be disappointed in the results until we'd finished the series. I figured we could cross that bridge when we came to it. In the meantime, I held out hope that we'd see improvement after injection number three.

We decided I would call the neurologist and talk it over with him. On the phone the next day, he told me he understood our concerns about the injections not working. He also said a lot of things I didn't totally understand. I got the gist, though. Basically, he recommended we go ahead with the third injection since the existing research only showed successful outcomes after three. He couldn't really say if just one or two would help. I relayed this to Brad that evening, and we put our third injection appointment on the calendar.

A few weeks later, we took her to the specialist for the third time, then brought her home and helped her feel as comfortable as possible while she recovered. I hoped we'd see some improvement soon.

Bad Friend

I booked our hotels in Rome and Sorrento," I reported to Brad as I skipped down the basement staircase, holding my phone. Dakota stayed on the main level, blocked from the stairs by a gate I'd leaned against the wall.

"Nice!" Brad scooted up on the couch, gripping his game controller with both hands.

He and I were both stressed at work, so our vacation to Italy couldn't come soon enough. Brad was working with a new attending physician every month, which meant having to constantly adjust his schedule and navigate different personalities, work styles, and expectations. Sometimes, he was on call and needed to stay at the hospital overnight. Other times, he had to wake up early and drive to DC or Virginia. He was subsisting on energy drinks, protein bars, and the sweet relief of weekly video game sessions.

And me? I was at a particularly high level of frustration at work. I didn't know how to gain control of our department's strategic planning, or how to stop taking on all the additional technical tasks that weren't part of my skill set or my job description. I ended up spending the better part of my workdays trying to solve web coding and database problems. Did I go to school for that, sign up to do that, or have any interest in learning it? No. My degrees are in communications and public relations. My skills are writing, marketing, and working with donors. But I'd created a situation I couldn't get out of.

Luckily, it was almost March, which meant Brad and I would soon be relaxing and eating authentic Italian pizza and pasta. I could almost taste the tomatoes and feel the resulting canker sores. *Worth it.*

Brad paused his game and watched me sit down on the other end of the couch, tucking one leg under my butt. "I started making a mental list of the sights I want to see," he said. "Obviously the Colosseum, the Pantheon, the Vatican, the Roman Forum, and maybe we can do a day trip to Pompeii."

"I need to make sure Jess can watch the animals," I blurted out, remembering that I hadn't yet. I turned my phone over and opened my messaging app, then realized I couldn't easily type out a message right then—without the exact dates in front of me—so I set my phone on the arm of the futon.

I couldn't believe I'd waited so long to look for a pet sitter. And once I'd thought of it, I couldn't indulge in a conversation about all the sights we'd visit—not until I secured someone to watch the animals.

When we'd moved to Maryland from Colorado two years prior, I'd worried I wouldn't be able to find anyone I trusted to care for Dakota when we were traveling. Sidney was easy. Since he didn't go outside, I didn't worry much about his safety. When it came to Dakota, though, I could be hesitant to trust people. They had to be assertive enough to hold her leash tightly and be wary of potential threats to her safety, like squirrels or rabbits that could cause her to suddenly yank on the leash and take off. They also had to be gentle enough to walk slowly with her, keep an eye on her, and make sure she was comfortable and happy. And they had to be responsible and experienced enough to give her pills twice a day.

In Colorado, we had my friend Kim and two others, Robin and Hana, all people who were trustworthy, loved our animals, and helped me out of a bind more than once or twice, including the time I had to drop everything and take a red-eye flight to Texas when Brad was in the ICU. After moving to Maryland, I was glad to meet Jess through a mutual acquaintance, and I was relieved when she'd offered to watch our animals the first time we took a trip from our new home base. Jess quickly went from pet sitter to good friend.

I stood up from the futon and grabbed my phone.

"Do you have a backup in case Jess can't do it?" Brad asked.

I thought for a moment. "I'm not sure. Maybe Patty?" My friend Patty had watched the animals once before while Brad and I were on a short vacation. She was responsible and communicative. I knew she'd be a great option if Jess couldn't do it. But there was one problem. "It's been a while since I've talked to her," I confessed to Brad.

"How come?" he asked, his eyes following me as I walked toward the staircase.

"We just haven't hung out in a while. Nothing happened or anything. We're friends on Instagram."

Brad chuckled and returned his gaze to his game on the TV.

I walked up the stairs with a mission. At the top, I set the gate aside and left it propped up against the wall. We only needed to put it in front of the stairs when I was in the basement, since Dakota only tried to go downstairs when I did. From her bed in the living room, she looked up to see where I'd go next. "Hi, pup," I said as I strode down the hall to my office. She followed. I opened my laptop and found the dates of our trip, then opened the messaging app on my computer and typed the following to Jess:

> Hey! We're off to Italy next month, and I was wondering if you'd be willing and able to watch the animals for us. It'd be March 9–17. Dakota takes two pills now, but you know these beasts, they're pretty easy. We would pay you, whether you like it or not.

After just a few seconds, my laptop dinged. I hoped like heck Jess could bail me out of what would otherwise become a stressful endeavor—either to message Patty or to find an entirely new person. I clicked to read Jess's reply:

> How exciting! I'll actually be out of town then too.

There was more to her message, but I stopped reading at that point. *Dammit. Now what?* I opened Instagram, clicked on Patty's profile, and then closed it. I couldn't bring myself to ask her for a favor after not having seen or talked to her in several months. We didn't have a falling out or anything—not in the slightest—but it still just seemed wrong. Instead, I searched the Internet for pet sitting companies in the area. There were some that specialized in cats, but it would be hard for me to trust them with Dakota. There was one that looked great but was booked through April. There were a few others who offered two visits per day, which flabbergasted me. *Who goes a full day only needing to pee twice?*

Against my better judgment, I messaged Patty.

> Hey, Patty! I hope you've been well. We should get together soon! I'm writing now bc Brad and I are going on vacation March 9–17, and I'm wondering if you'd be free to watch the animals. It would mean staying at our house, and we would pay you, of course. Let me know if you're open to it!

For the next two days, I checked Instagram, hoping to see a reply. I worried that my bad friendship had appalled Patty. I could picture her reading my message over and over, seething and thinking to herself that I was a terrible person. I was sure she was working hard to brainstorm a reply that would put me in my place. *Ugh. Why did I message her?*

On the third day, a notification popped up with Patty's name on it. My posture went from bad to worse as I read her message. It wasn't unkind, but she gave it to me straight. She told me it didn't feel good to finally hear from me only because I needed something from her, so she wasn't going to watch the animals for me. I felt like sinking into the floorboards and living the rest of my life in the dark, spiderwebby crawl space under our house. Sure, I hadn't fallen out of touch with her intentionally, but I'd had the nerve to message her out of the blue to ask her to work for me. *Gross, Lisa.* She was right to be upset. I felt like the worst friend in history. Not only that but I also felt like a bad pet owner. A good one would've made such plans months earlier. Our trip was less than a month away, and I had nobody to take care of Dakota and Sidney.

I went to the kitchen to take a break and find a snack—to eat my feelings. Dakota followed, hoping for a snack of her own. When I passed the stairs before entering the kitchen, I yelled down to Brad, who was watching TV between reading chapters in a medical textbook. "Hey, Brad!"

"What?!" he yelled back, sounding irritated. I stepped down to the landing so he could hear me better.

"Jess and Patty both said no to pet sitting."

Brad paused the TV. "Wha'd you say?" he called up to me.

"Both my pet sitters said no!" I shouted down to him.

"Womp, womp," he interjected.

"And Patty's pretty pissed at me for even asking."

"Uh-oh. Wha'd she say?" Brad asked, concerned for my feelings and ready to take my side.

"Oh, just that I'm a total scumbag and should never speak to the likes of her again."

"Did you tell her you're sorry you're a scumbag?" Brad joked.

"Yeah, I said, 'I'm sorry. *Now* will you watch my animals?'" I joked back.

"Ha ha," he said, ending our exchange.

In the kitchen, I snagged a treat for Dakota and a small bag of Sour Patch Kids for myself. She chewed the treat just outside the kitchen, dropping crumbs on the sunroom rug. She licked up each one, leaving a clean space behind her as she followed me and the Sour Patch Kids back into my office.

I got back on Instagram and posted a request for pet sitter recommendations. Dakota sat beside my chair, staring at me. "No, puppy, go lay in your bed," I told her and turned back to the screen, scrolling through social media pages and my work inbox while I waited. I received messages from a few friends volunteering to pet sit, but none of them passed my tests. Some were cat people. Others were people I didn't think would want to stay at my house for ten days, either because they lived far away, had animals of their own, or had kids to worry about. One person was someone I found trustworthy, but I'd never seen her interact with animals at all. To me, it seemed weird that she'd even volunteer. A few people commented on my post, tagging their friends who did pet sitting. Knowing someone's name isn't enough for me to think I can trust them, though. *Why even bother?*

I sat back and swished a piece of candy in my mouth. I puckered my lips, wrinkled my nose, and squinted at its sourness. Swallowing the candy, I sat back up and refreshed my screen. Finally accepting that she wasn't getting any candy, Dakota lay down in her bed.

Just then, another message popped up on Instagram. When I saw who the sender was, I thought it was odd. It was a guy I'd done improv with once or twice in St. Louis. We hadn't interacted in a while, but he told me about his friend Cameron, who had recently moved to the DC area and had been dog sitting for two years. He sent me a link to Cameron's account on Rover and suggested I reach out to see if he was available. *At least he gave me more than just a name,* I thought. But I was still skeptical. I have a higher bar for pet sitters than most people I know. I tend to find something wrong with almost everyone, especially recommendations from people I barely knew through the improv community in St. Louis six years prior.

But looking at Cameron's profile, I started to let myself become hopeful. *Dog lover: check. Works from home: check. No* kids: check. *Works as a fraud investigator:* trustworthiness *check.* I connected with him, and we messaged back and forth with all the specifics. It was settled. I had a live-in pet sitter during my vacation. Crisis averted.

Just as I was feeling some relief, I caught sight of Dakota out of the corner of my eye. She had gotten up from her bed, and the base of her tail was moving up and down, a warning sign that she was about to poop. We called it "tail pumping" because her tail would lift an inch or two and then go back down, like a pump.

I jumped up from my chair and led her by the collar out of the room. But it was too late. As she ambled down the hall, through the kitchen, and into the sunroom, she left a trail of small, round nuggets behind her.

I opened the back door for her in case she needed to pee, then I hopscotched back into the kitchen, careful to avoid the fresh land mines. I reached into the basket atop our fridge, grabbed the edge of a poop bag, tore it off the roll, then palmed the paper towel roll from the cabinet underneath the sink. Since Dakota had started becoming more accident-prone, we'd started keeping extra paper towels in there along with two kinds of rug cleaner: one organic, one extra strength. I chose the latter. As I scanned the floor and collected all the nuggets, I made a note to myself to warn the pet sitter that Dakota might poop inside.

In Italy, Brad and I each got a much-needed break from work. We walked dozens of miles and saw famous historical sights. Brad taught me all about the Roman Forum as we walked around it and I snapped pictures. We took a selfie in the

Colosseum. We explored Pompeii and meowed at the stray cats that had taken up residence there. We ate pasta and pizza and gelato. We drank limoncello, and Brad finished mine. At the Capitoline Museums in Rome, I took a picture of the *Statue of a Dog* and posted it on social media that evening with the caption:

I miss Dakota.

Cameron didn't check in as often as we would've liked, but he kept Dakota and Sidney alive and safe.

A couple of weeks after her third injection, it became obvious that Dakota wouldn't be in the one in three dogs who benefit from epidural steroid injections. We'd seen no improvement after the first or second shots, and after the third one, we had our answer. Brad wasn't surprised. He had already come to that conclusion and experienced his disappointment. For me, it was just sinking in. I should've known. One in three odds aren't exactly a sure bet. But all my life, things had a tendency to work out for me. If there was luck to be had, it usually came my way. I'm usually the one out of three, and I had assumed Dakota would be too. But she wasn't.

I've asked myself since then if doing the injections was the right decision. Would I do things differently if I had a second chance? I still don't have an answer, and I don't think there is one. When you're making health-care decisions, whether for yourself or others, I don't think there's a clear right or wrong answer. You listen to the medical professionals and then weigh all the competing priorities and decide what's best. That's what we did, and I feel good about it.

Still, it was disheartening and disappointing that the steroids didn't help.

We still had physical therapy appointments every two weeks, and we still had the option of Dakota having the surgery. I was nowhere near the point of giving up.

Goodbye #6

After Lady #3 (the last one, I swear), my mom adopted a tiny white puppy with brown patches. Within days, we found out she had a congenital heart condition. She became paralyzed very quickly after we brought her home, and, because the paralysis was ascending, it was only a matter of time before it would stop her heart.

I rode with my mom and my best friend, Wendy, to the animal shelter, where we dropped off the puppy to be euthanized. I was fifteen. I hadn't yet worked in an animal shelter, so I didn't have opinions about dropping dogs off at one. I don't think I even knew there were choices about that.

Her name was Bella, but she wasn't with us long enough for her to learn it.

Car Accident

As I gripped the bottom of the steering wheel with my left hand, I held my phone in my right. Using only my thumb, I typed:

g

I glanced up at the road and back down. It was a Wednesday morning, and traffic was heavy.

a

Another quick glance up.

s

My phone autofilled the rest:

gas stations nearby

I hit enter and chose the first option, a Shell station a mile and a half away in Adelphi. There was no way this was the closest one, but it'd have to do. I couldn't keep messing with my phone and drive safely at the same time.

"It's okay, puppy." I cracked the windows and looked at Dakota in the rearview mirror. Somewhere between exits 27 and 29, she had pooped in the back seat. I'd asked her to lie down, but she hadn't. Since her balance wasn't great in the car, the slight strain of trying to remain on all fours had pushed out the poop.

At one point, I had considered putting Dakota in diapers to keep poop from getting on our rugs, something that had become a common occurrence. From what I'd heard, though, diapers would've only made a bigger mess by smooshing the poop into Dakota's fur, causing her discomfort, and possibly leading to infections. Not to mention that it would be a grosser mess to clean up. I'm not knocking doggy diapers; they work for a lot of dogs. But I'll take a pile of solid poop over smooshed poop embedded in dog fur any day.

For a while I had tried establishing a schedule for Dakota's eating, hoping that would create a more predictable bathroom routine. Up to that point, she had enjoyed unfettered access to her food. Each morning, I'd dump a big red cup of kibble into her bowl, and she'd eat it whenever she wanted to, usually grazing throughout the day. She was a maniac for treats, but she never overate her kibble. It wasn't exciting enough to cause "food brain." I guess we should've called it "treat brain."

When I started giving Dakota food just twice a day, she wouldn't eat it in a timely manner, so I had to put fish oil on it to entice her. Each morning and evening, I'd shake out a capsule from the plastic bottle, poke a hole in it with the pointy end of a corn-on-the-cob holder, and squeeze the fish oil onto the kibble. Did I know that fish oil also comes in, you know, *oil* form? Yes, but I had already purchased the capsules, so that's what I was going to use. And it worked. Kind of.

Dakota would eat her food right away . . . some of her food . . . the top layer . . . the part with the fish oil on it. After deeming that experiment a failure, I reverted to leaving food out for her all day and concentrated instead on being more proactive about taking her outside. But it wasn't always successful. I had taken her outside before we left the house that Wednesday morning but she wasn't interested in pooping.

Dakota stood, crouched in the back seat, trying to balance. As usual, her eyebrows and gray muzzle made her look worried and wise. The position of her ears—pulled down and away from her face, as if loosely pinned to the sides of her head—made her look so innocent and worried, like she was asking me what to do. She didn't want to step in the poop, but I couldn't help her until we pulled over—in four minutes, according to my phone's map.

"It's okay," I repeated. "We'll fix it."

I knew that if I had to hit the brakes hard, Dakota would lose her balance, so I tried to drive as steadily as possible, slowing down early for turns.

We were on our way to a physical therapy appointment. It was June, and we'd been going there every other week since February. I should've known by then that if she didn't poop before we left the house, she'd do it after we took off. She'd pooped in the lobby of the specialist's office twice at this point, and, while Dakota seemed unfazed, I was a little embarrassed. I thought it made her seem worse off than she actually was. I didn't want anyone to pity her, and I didn't want them to think she wasn't house-trained. *She's an old, happy dog with a responsible, caring owner. That's all. Mind your own business.*

I spotted the gas station on my right and pulled up by one of the available pumps. Then I opened the back left door and looked at Dakota. *She did step in it.* "It's okay, Peepers. We'll getcha cleaned up."

I hooked the leash to her collar, lifted her out, and set her on the ground. The mess was on the right side of the back seat so I ushered her around the back of the car to that side.

By this point in time, I kept a roll of paper towels and cleaning spray in my car, so I reached underneath the seat cover and retrieved them from the floorboard. I cleaned off Dakota's fur, taking my time with it and handling Dakota gently. *We're gonna be so late*, I fretted. *I hope they can still see us when we get there. It would be such a bummer to miss an appointment when they're so hard to get in the first place and we've already gone through all this trouble.*

I grabbed a poop bag from my purse, and while holding the leash with one hand, I cleaned the mess with the other. I felt like I needed to rush this part of the cleanup since Dakota was waiting behind me. I knew her back legs would be slowly giving out beneath her. Plus, I didn't feel entirely comfortable keeping her there with the leash but not being able to watch over her. I kept interrupting my cleanup to turn around and make sure she was okay. What a sight we must've been to the people getting their midmorning coffee and gas.

Following my cleanup job, I placed an old towel over the wet spot in the back seat. After giving Dakota a boost into the car, I got back in too.

"There. All fixed," I said to her. As we left the gas station, I grabbed my phone and pulled up the specialist's phone number. "We're running late," I told the receptionist over the Bluetooth. "We had a little accident in the car."

When the receptionist responded with shock and concern, I clarified, "Oh, no, we're fine! Not *that* kind of accident." I smiled at Dakota, who was clean and sitting comfortably on the back seat. Now *she sits!*

Summer came and went. Over the Fourth of July weekend, I discovered a silver lining to Dakota's old age: when the neighbors shot off fireworks, she slept right through it. A few times in the months before that, I had questioned whether she was losing her hearing. I'd leave a room, and she wouldn't follow me. Or she'd hear a noise on the TV and bark like it was someone at our front door. But she never had a problem hearing rustling bags of chips and dog treats. Nevertheless, the lack of reaction to fireworks made it clear that her hearing was diminished. (Sidney, whose hearing was fine, hid in the basement all night.)

While we continued taking Dakota to physical therapy, our faith in that also began to wane. Her mobility kept decreasing. Accidents in the house had become a regular part of our lives, as had occasional falls and her nails scraping on the concrete when we went for walks. She had gotten even slower getting up from lying down too.

Since I had work and the clinic only offered PT twice a week, it was hard to get in. But I kept going, thinking that we'd see less scraping and slipping on walks—or at least not *more*. But I was running out of hope.

Kindness

I sat with my left leg crossed on top of my right and a white cloth napkin draped over my lap. I pressed the seam of the tablecloth against my knee under the table, folding it over and back with my thumb and pointer finger. Noticing that I'd subconsciously tensed up my left ankle and toes, I quickly let my foot drop. *I'm very chill.*

Brad sat across the table from me, scanning the laminated menu in front of him. He flicked the frayed corner of the plastic with his thumb, making a satisfying *thwap* sound each time. *So not chill.*

He pushed off the floor with his feet, scooting his chair back from the table a few inches. "Ah, I don't know," he said. "I already told you that surgery isn't a cure-all. There's *always* a risk of side effects."

We'd talked about surgery back in January, when we first got Dakota's MRI results. Brad was against it from the start, and I was okay with leaving it as a last resort. I'd been okay with crossing that bridge when we came to it, and now it was in our sights. We'd tried the steroid injections, and I'd been taking her for physical therapy every two weeks. At this point, it was September, and we still hadn't seen any signs of improvement. In fact, it seemed like her spine issue had been progressively getting worse since we'd started all these treatments. It was probably just a matter of frequency illusion—when you notice something more often after noticing it a first time—but it scared me nonetheless.

I wanted to talk about surgery. I trusted Brad's medical knowledge and I valued his opinion, but I wanted another chance to understand where he was coming from and to go over all the options again. At the same time, I knew Brad didn't want to talk about it. He felt like we'd already discussed it thoroughly enough and settled on a decision not to do surgery. He had no interest in rehashing everything.

"I mean, it's a lot to put her through physically," Brad continued, knowing I wanted more of an explanation than he'd given me.

"Yeah," I said, not really agreeing, but listening and trying to understand. I held my red plastic soda cup in both palms. I took a sip, grabbing a chunk of ice with my top lip. I crunched the ice in the back of my mouth and put my right hand back under the tablecloth to fidget with it again.

"And mentally, right?" Brad added. "Best case scenario, even if the surgery actually fixed her stenosis, she'd still have to go through recovery and rehab, and that's like two months minimum."

"Right. That would suck." I wanted to agree with him. I really did. And on some level, I think I *did* agree. But I was slow to process it. I needed him to explain it in a way that would get through and make me understand. It reminded me of conversations I have every so often with my friend Leah. She's a compassionate person, an activist, knowledgeable about various social justice issues. I can reach out to her anytime I have a question about an issue I'm not familiar with—or when I catch myself feeling defensive or closed-off to new information. Most times I connect with her, it's because I've identified an area where I can grow and improve as a person or as an activist. Usually, I go into the conversations wanting her to explain to me why I'm wrong about something. That's how I felt talking to Brad about the surgery for Dakota. I needed the debate—not for the sake of proving I was right but rather to understand why I might not be.

"We also need to consider her age," Brad continued.

Nope. We don't. You're losing me. Know your audience, pal.

"Not because that determines whether she's 'worth it,'" he said, using air quotes.

Okay, I'm listening. Brad and I have a shared disdain for people who think it's a bad idea to spend money on health care for an older dog.

"Her age matters because . . . ," he paused before finishing his thought. "Because we're deciding how she'll spend the rest of her time."

Yep. Okay. That got through. I had never thought of it that way before. I had been closed-off to talking about her age in the context of these medical decisions because the only way I'd heard that done was, in my opinion, cruel and unfair, with people saying they weren't opting to spend money to fix their pets' health problems because they're already whatever age. As if they had a cutoff point, after which their pets were too old to deserve the best chance at a good, long life. But Brad was saying that Dakota's age matters for a different, compassionate reason—that because she was older, we had even more of a responsibility to make sure our decisions gave her the best life possible.

"Vegan chimichanga?" The server appeared next to our table, holding two hot plates of food.

"That's me." I raised my hand.

He set it down on the table in front of me, then put Brad's burrito down at his place setting.

"Thank you," I smiled up at him.

The conversation about surgery faded into mariachi music and polite dinner conversation, and, before I knew it, Brad and I were full and tired and on our way home.

We returned home to Dakota asleep in her bed in our bedroom, not having heard us come in. I grazed the back of her neck with my fingers to let her know we were home. She looked up at me and stretched all four legs. "Hi, Peepers," I said. "You wanna go outside?"

As I stood on the deck and watched Dakota sniff out a spot to pee, I thought about my responsibility to her. I had always considered myself someone who would do anything for her dog: whatever she needed, whenever she needed it. No amount was too much to spend. No inconvenience was too burdensome to bear. I'd feed her my last french fry from the dumpster.

For fourteen years, she had been a huge part of our family—of my identity. We'd never been married without her. I'd never been an adult without her. We'd shaped our lives around her, spent time house-training her, teaching her tricks, taking her for walks. We'd moved across the country together, from North Carolina to California, then back, to Illinois, Colorado, and Maryland. We'd taken her on road trips. We'd shared our food with her. She kept me company while I worked from home, and she was always there when I wanted to take a break for some sunshine or a walk around the block.

When I was sad, I sat on the floor by her bed and pet her neck. When Brad and I had uncomfortable conversations, we could look at her instead of at each other. We could break the tension by speaking in her voice or by laughing at something silly she'd done, like demanding treats as a reward after playing with Brad.

I desperately wanted there to be a solution, and I let myself think surgery was it. I wanted to fix Dakota's spine, not lessen her symptoms or make her more comfortable. I wanted a cure-all. But the truth is that there wasn't a solution. Not a good one, anyway. Not a safe one, a sure one, a kind one.

Brad helped me see the nuances involved in deciding how to care for someone. It's not always best to do whatever it takes to *solve their problem*. Sometimes the side effects and potential risks actually make that a less kind option. Sometimes, what's best for the dog is for their owner to accept the harsh reality that losing them, eventually, is inevitable. To focus on making the most of the time you have, knowing that no matter how long it lasts, it will never be enough. To stop trying to keep them here forever and instead do whatever it takes to love them as much as possible while they're here.

And so, it was decided. We wouldn't put Dakota through a surgery, and we also wouldn't make her continue going to physical therapy appointments that were hard on her, a pain for me, and didn't seem to be helping. Instead, we would shift our focus toward maintaining her quality of life. That was the best and kindest option. Of course, that didn't make it any less scary.

Burnout

Dakota rose from her bed and made her way toward me, stopping about two feet from where I sat, hunched over my computer on the coffee table in front of me. I was focused on my laptop screen, but in my peripheral vision, I saw her staring at me. "Okay, hold on." She needed to go outside.

Dakota shuffled her feet and wagged her tail just enough for the end to swing a couple of times. Just enough that she knew I could see it.

"Hold on," I repeated, glancing at her so she knew I was acknowledging her need. She could wait a minute. She had trouble controlling her bowel movements but had full bladder control. In fact, most times she asked to go outside as if it were an emergency, but when we got out there, she lollygagged and smelled the air for a while before actually doing her business.

I needed to finish the email I was working on. A donor had asked me a question, so I had to spend my precious time crafting a response that would explain the answer with just the right amount of information—enough to answer his question in a satisfying manner but not with so much detail that I'd invite even more questions. I didn't have time for that.

"Rrrff," Dakota barked softly, using her inside voice—the one reserved for asking politely and for quietly warning us in bed about noises she heard outside that were probably nothing but might be something.

"Wait," I said impatiently. *Jesus, dog. Give me one second.*

"Owrrr!" she cried, louder than the bark.

At that point, I snapped. "Wait!" I shouted at her, emphasizing both consonants and making each one into a weapon. It was the yell of someone who was fed up . . . burnt out . . . spent.

In a single motion, Dakota lay down right where she'd been standing.

I froze. I immediately regretted yelling at her and wished I could take it back. I was like one of those abusive men in Lifetime movies. The ones who hit their girlfriends and then immediately apologize, begging for forgiveness and professing their love.

If this were a scene in a movie, the camera would pull back sharply and dramatically, exposing the entire room: me, sitting on the edge of the couch cushion, eyes wide, tears welling up in them; Dakota, lying on the rug in front of me, innocent and confused about what she'd done wrong. Then it would cut to a close-up shot of her face, with the eyebrows I loved so much. Next, a close-up of my face, dumbfounded at the realization that I was the villain.

I felt taken aback, disgusted by my actions, lost. I'd veered so far off track that I didn't recognize myself. Up until then, I hadn't even noticed that I was straying off course. It must have been slow and sneaky. But there I was—or whoever this was—this person who would yell at her dog, her best friend. A person who was so mixed up that she prioritized an insignificant work email over Dakota. I didn't even know why I felt rushed. My work wasn't time sensitive. Nobody was rushing me except myself.

I pushed my laptop back a few inches on the coffee table and stood up. Dakota stood too.

I walked over to her and kneeled in front of her. Cupping my hands on the sides of her neck, I gently pulled her face toward mine and rubbed my thumbs just below her ears. "I'm sorry, puppy. I'm so sorry I yelled. C'mon, let's go outside."

Out back, Dakota stood on the top of the ramp, sniffing at the wind. I sat on the edge of the deck and watched as she sauntered down the ramps and into the yard, then I let my head fall into my arms. I didn't know how to fix this problem. *What happened to me? I used to be so easygoing, but now anytime I get stressed at work, it's like a switch flips in my nervous system. My face grows hot, my limbs grow cold, and I feel trapped, as if gravity has gone into overdrive and I'm being slowly crushed into the floor by an invisible human trash compactor. Instead of pausing, collecting myself, and dealing with my emotions, I lash out at others? If I'm not crying at inopportune times, I'm making sarcastic, passive-aggressive remarks to innocent coworkers. And now I've apparently stooped to yelling at my best friend. I deserve to be squashed in a trash compactor.*

Throughout her life, I had asked so much of Dakota. I'd moved her back and forth across the country five times. I'd given her a big backyard to run in and then taken it away. I'd asked her for patience and understanding when I had to leave for eight hours a day to work in offices. I expected good behavior from her. I'd asked for her companionship and protection, especially when Brad couldn't be there. When he was in Iraq, at work, or busy with school or training, I could always turn to Dakota. If I was lazy, she'd be lazy with me. If I was sad, she'd let me pet her and cry to her, and she'd make me feel better, just by being present. When I was by myself, she reminded me that I actually wasn't. She stood, barking, between me and strangers on the street and knocks at the front door. She had never once let me down. Never. And here I was, doing that to her.

I couldn't be that person. It's not who Dakota deserved. Something needed to change.

Quality of Life

E ven as I waited for the pages to print and the ink to dry, I told myself I didn't need the form yet. I'd downloaded it from the website of Lap of Love, a company my friend told me about after using its in-home euthanasia service for her dog who'd been ill. The company had great resources for people with aging dogs: a pet hospice journal, guidance on how to know when it's time to say goodbye, and a form for measuring your dog's quality of life. In a huff I snatched ten copies of the latter from my printer, as if I hadn't been the one who'd decided to print them in the first place. As resistant as I was, I also knew that when it came time to think about those things, it would be helpful to see the trends over time.

The form had spaces for dog owners to fill in with numerical measurements for things like mobility and appetite. The scale started at two, which meant things were going well. A score of one was for mild issues, and zero was the worst score, indicating problems like bare minimum mobility and showing no interest in favorite things.

I penned the date at the top:

October 19, 2019

I listed everything as a two except for mobility, which I put as a one. According to the scale, a one for mobility was defined as:

Difficulty getting up, hard to get in position to eliminate, short walks only

There. Done. I hope you're happy, I said in my head to an invisible villain.

Needing to switch gears to something more positive, I stood up from my office chair and set the papers aside on my desk. I paused at the doorway to supervise Dakota as she got up from her bed to follow me. "You got it?" I asked, ready to assist if she needed help. She pushed off the floor with her front feet. Once. Twice. On the third time, she had enough momentum to lift her body. One more try and I would've done it for her. It was hard to watch her struggle.

I walked down the hall and meandered through the living room, dining room, and sunroom. I did my best to keep my head up and not glance around too much, but Dakota was onto me. She followed me closely, her mouth open and stretched wide like a smile. Her ears sat high on her head, signaling that she saw through my feigned nonchalance and knew exactly what I was looking for.

After spotting it in the corner by Sidney's cat tree, I asked the question Dakota had been waiting for: "Where's your Kong?"

Dakota's eyes darted around the room. When she spotted it, she trotted over and picked it up with her mouth, then tossed it back onto the floor. "Bring it here, nerd," I said. She picked it up a second time and tossed it again, this time in my direction. Standing ready, I cupped my hands together in front of my knees and caught it. "Good girl! Do you want treats in your Kong?" What a ridiculous question. Of course she did. Kongs filled with peanut butter were still Dakota's favorite thing. I only asked the question to get her even more excited.

I grabbed the jar of peanut butter with the stick figure of a dog drawn on the lid. The other jar was for humans. I put a glob of peanut butter and a few crunchy treats in the Kong while Dakota lay just outside the kitchen watching me, wide-eyed with anticipation.

Back when she was a puppy, I'd ask Dakota where her Kong was and then go look for it, expecting some help from her to find it. Not only would she not help, she'd follow me around with urgency, watching me, wondering why I wasn't finding it. She couldn't think straight. She had "food brain."

Dakota's excitement over treats was one of the only things that hadn't changed in her fourteen years on planet Earth. She didn't play with toys anymore, and she was over Nylabones, but she'd loved Kongs filled with peanut butter her whole life. I thought about the form I had printed and about reducing Dakota's life to mere numbers on a form. *If she still loves Kongs—if she still finds joy—do these quality-of-life scores even matter?* I asked myself. I understood by now that the length of Dakota's life shouldn't be the only measure of my success as a dog owner—that the quality of her time was the more important factor. *But how do I measure quality?* Thinking about it logically—mathematically—any amount of joy is greater than *none*, which is the amount you can experience if you're not alive. *Even if someone only experiences happiness 5 percent of the time, isn't that better than 0 percent? Isn't being alive always better than not?*

These questions swirled through my mind, but I didn't have to figure out my answer quite yet. Dakota wasn't anywhere near as low as 5 percent happiness. She still found joy in a lot of things: getting pet on the back of her neck, exploring the backyard, eating things she shouldn't, taking walks around the neighborhood (and eating things she shouldn't), good smells, all treats, and especially peanut butter Kongs.

"Here ya go," I said as I handed her the Kong.

She grabbed it with her teeth and carried it into the living room as I followed. I wanted to be there when she inevitably lay down in a weird position and needed help getting back up. In her old age, Dakota had begun to misjudge where her back end would fall when lying down on a bed, so she'd end up with her butt hanging off the side and her legs akimbo. Or she'd lie on the tiny patches of hardwood left uncovered, or on our thin living room rug, and with the weakness in her legs she couldn't get the leverage to hoist herself back up.

I watched Dakota as she licked the peanut butter she could reach and squeezed the Kong in her jaw to break up the pieces of treat I'd put in there for her. Anytime a piece fell out, she grabbed it, lifted her head, and chewed it proudly.

"Good job." I smiled at her. *This is quality of life.*

After a few minutes, I helped her get up from lying in her unusual position. "Let's go over here," I suggested, picking up the Kong, which was slimy with dog spit, and carried it with my thumb and middle finger into the carpeted sunroom. The carpet there was thicker and therefore less slippery than the living room rug.

Dakota followed me, watching the Kong in my hand, eager to reunite with it. Once she lay down on the carpet, I darted back into my office and returned to the sunroom with my laptop. *Time to do something about my own quality of life*, I thought as I sat on the sunroom carpet next to Dakota. I moved my cursor to the address bar and typed:

id

The browser filled in the rest:

Idealist.org

I hit enter and was glad to see that there were new postings since I'd checked that morning.

I had officially resigned from my job a week prior. In my letter, I'd thanked Mike for all the opportunities and offered up to two months' notice before I'd be gone. If I found a job that required me to start sooner than that, I'd let him know and do everything I could to help with a smooth transition. Even though I didn't have a new job lined up—or even any serious prospects—I needed to use my network to look for my next job. And in order to do so without fear that word would get back to him, I'd had to tell my current boss I was planning to leave. I fretted over it for days, assuming he would be upset with me for leaving. Instead, he handled it professionally and kindly. *Whew.*

I filtered the results to see only the remote jobs. After almost five years of working from home, I had no interest in going back to an office—especially with a senior dog who required care and supervision. I scrolled through the postings, scanning for keywords like *marketing, communications,* and *fundraising.*

Dakota's licking noises stopped and I looked up to see why. She had licked the Kong to where it was out of reach in front of her. I reached over and repositioned it between her front legs, and she went back to licking. I scrolled through job postings, not expecting to see anything that caught my eye. But to my surprise, one job stood out from the rest. It was for a nonprofit that helped people install solar panels and advocated for more access to solar energy. I liked having our solar panels and I do care about the environment, but I didn't feel particularly passionate about solar energy. I mean, I didn't go around telling people they should get solar panels, and I didn't know anything about the energy system or solar advocacy. But I thought that might be a welcomed change after spending the previous five years in a job that focused on my passion. It had been my dream job, but it had also burned me out pretty hard.

I clicked to read the full job description. *Whoa! They're looking for someone who can write marketing copy that isn't dry . . . that uses humor and reads like it was actually written by a human. My specialty!* It was a lower level than my current job, but maybe that was good too. It probably meant less responsibility—and, therefore, less stress. Even so, the salary far exceeded mine, which would be a nice bonus. I read on to see that I met all the qualifications, except for a couple of specific things that I could easily learn on the job. *This might be the perfect next step in my career.*

That night, I tweaked my résumé to fit the needs of the job and wrote a cover letter that I knew would impress. It totally sounded like a human wrote it, and I even incorporated some humor. I had fun writing it too, which I took to be a very good sign.

Goodbye #7

After a period of grieving for Bella, the puppy with the congenital heart condition, my mom was ready to get another dog. She bought a shih tzu puppy and named her Rascal.

I'm not sure why she decided to go to a breeder instead of adopting like she usually did. Maybe the puppy with the heart condition scared her, making her think that buying a dog would be more predictable than rescuing one.

Whatever the reason, once Rascal joined the family, the frequent goodbyes at our house came to an end. She lived with my parents for fifteen years.

One day in 2014, my mom texted me:

can I call you?

I said yes.

On the phone, her voice broke as she told me that Rascal had died. Hearing her cry made me cry too. My mom had finally had a dog for long enough, and bonded with her strongly enough, to be heartbroken when it was time to say goodbye. With my brother and me living on our own, Rascal had become her baby. Rascal was deaf, mostly blind, and had a sore on her foot that kept breaking open and bleeding, so my parents had made the decision that it was time.

I don't remember our conversation, but I'm sure I was awkward and silent and not comforting to talk to. I'm sure I had no idea what to say. I never do in such situations, and that one was particularly bad. My mom's heartbreak was something I could only imagine.

Nailing It

My phone alarm blared the theme song to *The West Wing* at 6:48 a.m. I scrambled to press the button and make the noise stop, then lay still for a few seconds to let my heartbeat return to normal. I was never awake that early.

It was November 4, my first day of work at the solar nonprofit. I had accepted the position a month earlier, and my previous boss, Mike, was supportive, providing me with a glowing recommendation during the hiring process and congratulating me when I shared that I'd gotten the job.

My new employer was headquartered in DC, and, though my position would be remote, my new manager, Shane, had asked me to come to the office for orientation my first week. That meant taking the Metro to Dupont Circle, which, together with the drive from my house to the closest Metro station and the short walk to the office, totaled an hour of travel time.

I looked over at Dakota sleeping soundly in her bed. Next to the bed stood a roll of paper towels and a red bottle of rug cleaner. I took a picture with my phone and texted it to Brad with the caption:

> you cleaned up poop four feet from my head
> and i didn't wake up? i'm amazing!

He wrote back:

> yeah, you're somethin else.

I chuckled. Sometimes Dakota would poop in her bed overnight. After waking up a few times to a hardened nugget or two on the rug by her bed, I had bought some pee pads and laid them out. Of course, then we never saw another one. We later learned, after waking up to the sound of smacking, that Dakota had started eating her poop. She'd never done that before, so we chalked it up to her either needing to "clean it up" so she could get back to sleep or to her becoming senile. We did what we could to prevent it, but it happened.

I was about to get out of bed when I saw Sidney stroll in. He meowed and trilled as he approached the bed then jumped up next to me and slinked onto to my chest. Like every morning, he purred into the crook of my neck while we snuggled for a few minutes before it was time for me to get up.

"Okay, kitty cat," I said after a few minutes. "I gotta get up." I twitched my shoulder to signal him to get off me, and he meowed and jumped down.

I stood up from my bed and leaned over Dakota, running my fingertips down her back. "Time to wake up, pup."

After she stretched and yawned, I supervised her exit from the bed, took her out back to pee, and then came inside to give her two pills with a spoonful of peanut butter. She followed me from room to room as I got ready, and she stood at the top of the stairs when I left for work. "Be good, dogs," I said, even though one was a cat.

I got to the office five minutes before my nine o'clock orientation. It was on the fourth floor of a huge building that took up half a block. On the first floor, there was a donut shop and a Panera, which I always call St. Louis Bread Company since that's what they're called there.

My boss, Shane, had already emailed me an agenda for the day. I met with him to talk about how we'd work together, and I sat in on some meetings to start learning the ropes. I was enjoying my first day, but I was also preoccupied thinking about Dakota. I had asked my friend Jess to come over that day to let her out, but it still made me nervous to leave Dakota alone. *She'll probably just sleep the whole time*, I told myself.

Shane treated me to lunch at the Bread Company downstairs, and I spent the afternoon in front of my computer, familiarizing myself with the platforms and tools I'd be using in my new job. All day, I kept being surprised by things that are fairly mundane but that I had forgotten about after five years of allowing my job to take over my life. I used a laptop that was provided to me, where I could keep work files and emails separate from personal ones on my own computer. Shane introduced me to the IT person, who would help me with the spreadsheets and HTML issues. And at five or five thirty, everyone quit for the day, leaving their laptops and papers on their desks.

After a grueling but promising orientation week, I happily settled in to a new routine at home. I worked from my home office most days, although I still occasionally ventured out to the couch, dining room table, or back deck. Every weekday, I closed my laptop at five thirty and declared myself done for the day. Truly done. Like, not even thinking about work anymore. My life and work were finally in balance.

Shane gave me ample feedback, which struck fear in my heart at first. He'd message me on Slack:

Hey, can I give you some feedback?

Here it comes, I'd think. *What did I do wrong this time? What's he gonna tell me I screwed up?* Whether or not it was accurate, I often felt like I was letting people down at my previous job. I couldn't handle the technical tasks. I took on too much and then resented it, and I think those feelings showed up in my communication with colleagues.

But Shane's feedback was almost always positive. It made me smile every time, and sometimes I even texted Brad or my parents to share the kind things my boss said about my work. It made me proud—and relieved to finally feel like I was doing well.

Since I wasn't as passionate about solar energy as I am about animal rights, I also wasn't as obsessive about work. I didn't really think about it during evenings or weekends. Instead, I used my off time to hang out with friends, walk Dakota without stressing, and bounce back from how burnt out I had been. I felt like I had time and space to think about things outside of work.

I don't remember what prompted it, but one day I got the idea that Dakota's nails might be longer than they should be. Maybe a Facebook friend had made a passive-aggressive comment on a photo I'd posted of Dakota. Or maybe I was just grasping at straws, looking for any possible aspect of Dakota's life that I had control over, that I could improve.

Wherever my concern came from, I decided to satisfy it with some quality, in-depth, academic research. Just kidding, I pulled up YouTube. I don't remember exactly what I typed in. Probably something brilliant and specific to start with, like:

trim dog nails

I know it sounds bad that I had a fourteen-year-old dog and I didn't know how to trim her nails. I could cut Sidney's, but it had to be done one nail at a time, in between copious amounts of head petting. But with Dakota, we'd never had to do it before. She used to wear her nails down on our walks, and if that didn't do the trick, she'd lie down on her side and pull at her nails with her teeth. That's right, she was once a nail biter like me. Like my father before me and his father before him. And I was relieved to not have to cut her nails for her. I have a clear memory of doing it once when she was seven months old, and it didn't go well.

We were in the middle of our move from North Carolina to California, and we had stopped in Illinois to visit our parents and to pick up some of our belongings from each of their houses. While staying with my mom and dad, we made use of their backyard hose to give Dakota a bath.

We had bathed her once before—in the bathtub of our apartment in North Carolina. I call it her baptism because it was, to my knowledge, her first bath. She shed so much that we realized it probably wasn't ideal for the pipes to bathe her in a tub.

After her hose bath in my parents' backyard, Brad and I dried her off with an old towel, ran her around to get out some of her energy, and then brought out the nail clippers.

Brad is a very tough guy. He can do a hundred pull-ups (I'm guessing). He can bench-press seven hundred pounds. (Okay, maybe I don't know anything about lifting weights; the point is that he's strong.) But when it comes to fingernails or, in this case, toenails, he's a straight-up baby. He won't help me cut the animals' nails, and he winces at the mere mention of anyone's nails being too short or bending or being cut. So my dad helped me. Well, he tried.

Some nail trimmers have a little safety guard that is meant to block the sharp portions when the trimmers aren't in use. It swivels out of the away once you're ready to clip your pet's nails. My dad thought the safety guard had a different purpose.

I stood over Dakota with her torso between my knees while my dad crouched down in front of her.

"You can cut all the way down to here," he instructed, pointing to the safety guard.

That didn't sound right to me. I thought the cut would be too deep. But he's my dad. As much as I tease him for "dadsplaining," he really does know a lot. So I assumed that he knew better than me.

I tightened my knees on either side of Dakota's body and held her paw in my hand. Then I lined up her nail with the safety guard and crunched down.

She winced and yelped.

I dropped my body onto hers and grabbed her whole paw with my hand. "Ahhh, I'm sorry! I'm so sorry!"

She was bleeding. *I'd* made her bleed. I didn't mean to, but I did it. It was my fault. I felt like I had betrayed her. In a way, I had also betrayed myself. I didn't feel good about what my dad had told me. Even though I trusted his intelligence and his ability to give spot-on advice, I didn't agree with him that particular time. I trusted him but not his idea. I didn't know how to interpret that feeling, but I knew I felt uneasy, and yet I squeezed the clippers anyway. I had such a lack of confidence in my own intelligence that I didn't even pause to consider what I knew to be true.

I held Dakota's paw tightly, applying pressure to where I had just injured it. And I held her close, apologizing, nearly in tears.

Move over in that crib, Brad. Now there are two straight-up babies.

Nearly fourteen years later, it's no wonder I didn't want to revisit the whole nail-trimming fiasco.

But Dakota needs me to, I thought. *Probably.... I guess I'm gonna find out.*

I set my laptop on the coffee table, lay down on the love seat, and chose one of the videos on YouTube that looked the most informational without being too boring. The dog in the first video had much shorter nails than Dakota, and I wondered if that was how short Dakota's nails should've been. *No, it can't be,* I decided. *All dogs are different, and besides, the person in the video is just a regular dog owner like me, not some expert in dog nails. Even if she were to say that dogs' nails should be that short, what does she know?*

I watched another video. Short nails again. *Hmm.* I sat for a few seconds with my fingers hovering above the keyboard. I cracked the knuckle of my pointer finger by bending it with my thumb. I moved my cursor back to the search bar and typed:

how long should dogs nails be

In the next video, the host—a veterinarian—said that a dog's nails shouldn't touch the floor when they walk. *Oh no. Dakota's do. And she's an old girl with mobility issues. What if not trimming her nails often enough contributed to her issues in the first place? How could I not know this basic fact about dog care? I trained her to sit, shake, stay, and leave it, but it never occurred to me to learn anything about nail trimming? I can't believe I've failed her again.*

Okay, get over it. Don't dwell. Now that I know better, as Maya Angelou would say, I just need to do *better.*

Next YouTube search:

how to trim thick black nails dog

I watched several videos. I learned that the word *quick* is spelled with a *c* in it, not "quik," which is what I'd thought for years. I felt like a failure in two areas of knowledge I valued: dog care *and* spelling.

I learned how to tell when you're close to the quick: If the end of your dog's nail looks white or light gray, you can trim a little bit more. If you see a small, shiny dot in the center of their nail, stop trimming.

I learned that you can't just clop off nails when they've been growing for fourteen and a half years, and you finally realize they're too long. The quick grows along with the nails, so you have to correct it over time.

I learned about a tool to use on dogs who aren't big fans of clippers: a Dremel.

That weekend, I made a trip to pick up one at the hardware store. I read the instructions while it charged, then sat down on the sunroom carpet with Dakota lying in front of me. She was skeptical but cooperative.

Every weekend after that, I'd sit with her in the same spot and sand down her nails little by little. Brad was even more skeptical than Dakota. He'd see me getting out the Dremel and treats and ask, "Again?"

"Yes. Again."

I had confidence in the knowledge I'd gained. Yeah, from YouTube. Don't judge. I was finally coming into my own. Trusting myself. Nailing this whole senior dog owner thing. Pun intended.

New Normal

B rad stood, bent over, holding Dakota's rear end in his arms. Her front legs balanced on the back seat of my car. "I got 'er, I got 'er."

I had just warned him that she would need help getting into the car. He had heard me, and he probably even believed me, but he wanted to see it for himself. So he had stood at the ready while she attempted to hop in, and he'd caught her midjump when it was clear that her back end wasn't going to make it. I knew she wasn't at risk of falling or getting hurt. If Brad said he had something covered, he meant it. Still, I had to stop myself from saying, "I told you so."

As I drove to the park, I thought about what lay ahead for Brad and smiled a knowing smile. Soon, he'd get to see how much different our dog park visits had become.

When Dakota was young, it was a challenge to bring her to the dog park. She'd pull on the leash, all the way from the car to the gate. She'd lunge forward and spring up and down on only her hind legs. We nicknamed it "kangarooing." What she was communicating was clear: "I want to get there faster!" But just in case the nonverbal cues weren't sufficiently getting her point across, she'd also whine and bark desperately at a volume that raised eyebrows and turned heads. I worried that park patrons would think we were bringing in an attack dog.

Once we'd make it through the gate, Dakota was very well behaved. She'd take off running as soon as we unhooked her leash and bound around joyfully, smelling every mouth and butthole she could get her nose on. Then, after discovering what every dog had eaten earlier that day, she'd check all the humans' hands and pockets for treats. Brad and I would stand by, watching all the fun and interjecting with the occasional "Dakota, don't jump!"

As she would run around from one dog to another, we'd joke that she had doggy ADHD. She didn't have the focus or drive for fetching, but she loved chasing dogs as *they* chased balls. Despite her speed, she never caught up to anyone. Three-fourths of the way there, she'd catch a whiff of something else she wanted to go smell and abandon her chase.

Dakota was always the first to notice each new dog who approached the park entrance, and she'd bolt over to the gate to greet them. She loved everyone she met. If she heard one dog barking at another, she'd run over to see what the problem was and get to the bottom of the dispute so they could all be friends again. Brad called her Henry Clay for how she seemed to mediate arguments. If you're not up on your American history, allow me to explain: Henry Clay, our nation's ninth secretary of state, earned the nickname the Great Compromiser. Like

Dakota, when he heard two dogs barking at each other in the Cabinet Room, he'd run over to see how he could help.

At one point, when we lived in California and Dakota was about two years old, we tried to train her to stop kangarooing into the park. We had taken her to a mostly worthless training course at a national pet store chain, and they were supposed to teach her not to pull on walks. Instead, they taught her a couple of irrelevant tricks and recommended a special collar we could buy to help prevent pulling. After that, we started our own do-it-yourself training program, determined to make it more pleasurable to walk with her.

Brad and I would get out of the car at the dog park and tell Dakota, still in the back seat, to sit. Once she did, we'd open the car door and start walking her toward the gate, which was on the opposite side of the park. As soon as she started kangarooing, we'd change directions and walk back toward the car. Changing directions suddenly is supposed to be a good way to prevent your dog from pulling on walks. Not only can it keep them guessing about which direction you're going, it can also show them that pulling won't get them where they want to go faster. You're essentially saying to your dog, "Don't mess with me, dog. I'm unhinged. I will waste my own time going *this* way when you and I both know we need to go *that* way!"

We'd try walking toward the gate, Dakota would start pulling again, and we'd head back the other way. On more than a few occasions, we spent more time trying to make it to the gate than we did playing in the park. Dakota seemed utterly confused by these shenanigans. *Why are we turning around? Why aren't we trying to get to the gate as quickly as possible for some fun at the park? What are you doing?* I'm sure she was thinking.

Don't mess with me, dog. I'm unhinged!

Dakota's stubbornness outlasted ours and our training eventually fizzled out. You can say we were being pushovers, but I prefer to think we were accepting our pup for who she was: a kangaroo.

When we arrived at the park, Brad lifted fourteen-year-old Dakota out of the car and set her on the asphalt. As we walked down the grassy hill toward the gate, he wrapped the end of her leash around his wrist. But Dakota's leash pulling days were long gone. While I had become accustomed to this calm, leisurely Dakota, it was still new to Brad. Usually, I would say something. I was always telling Brad how to do things when it came to Dakota. Pet care was an area in which I got Mario Brothers Syndrome a lot. But this time, I was a little excited to witness Brad discover for himself that holding the leash so tightly was no longer necessary.

I lingered behind him and Dakota, watching them walk side by side. It only took about fifteen steps before Brad unraveled the leash. He kept watching Dakota. I couldn't see his face, but I pictured a look of awe on it. He glanced back at me with a smile. I watched. He repositioned the leash, understanding that he could hold it with much more slack than he was accustomed to. He slowed to let me catch up to them, looked at me, and said, "I guess I don't need to hold the leash super tight anymore, huh?" We weren't happy that Dakota had less energy, of course. We were just smitten with how calmly she walked beside us.

As we entered the park, I heard a man's voice in front of us. "Looks like we've got ourselves an elder statesman here?" A tall, bearded man was smiling at Dakota. He was elderly himself.

"Yep," I glanced at him and smiled at Dakota. "She'll be fifteen next summer."

I didn't usually round up Dakota's age. I didn't want anyone to pity her—or me. And I didn't want to cheat her out of any remaining time. But I could tell this man didn't pity Dakota. On the contrary, he was in awe of her.

His eyes were lit up and his lips were stretched and open in a half smile, half jaw drop as he watched Dakota walk by.

She definitely looked old, with her white face and paws and scruffy fur and muscle loss. But she was also lean, mobile, and clearly happy to be there. That made me feel proud. It felt to me like evidence that I'd taken good care of her to get her to that point. But, more importantly, it brought me gratitude and hope for the time we had left with each other. If she was doing this well at fourteen and a half, maybe we had a long time left together. As we walked around the park, I glanced at the man again. He was still looking at Dakota and smiling.

Brad and I strolled along, following Dakota around the park. She smelled the other dogs, then the people's hands, then the grass under the trees at the back of the park. I hovered, ready to catch her if she tripped or to protect her if she found herself in the path of a puppy chase or a person's misstep.

At a stoplight on the drive home, Brad lowered the rearview mirror to gaze at Dakota in the back seat. Then he turned to me with a look in his eyes that meant he had an idea. "We should take her somewhere to see snow this winter."

Dakota loved snow. She found it fun to romp around in and even more fun to eat. "The ground is made of treats," we'd say on her behalf.

When it was snowy, she would ask to go outside just to snack on it. She loved catching snowballs Brad tossed to her, swallowing whatever portion made it into her mouth before it broke on impact with her snout. One time, after Dakota kept asking to go outside to eat snow, we put some in a plastic bowl and brought it inside for her. She shivered while finishing up every bite, then rested in front of our space heater.

"Okay!" I replied to Brad in our car. "I bet my new coworker would know some good places to go. She lives in West Virginia." I loved the idea of taking Dakota on a trip that was just for her. We could play in the snow, take her on walks, and give her yummy treats. It sounded fantastic.

We arrived home from the dog park about seven minutes after we'd left, and Brad lifted Dakota out of the car by the curb in front of our house. It took more time to get there and back than we'd spent at the park itself, but it was totally worth it. Not only did I get to watch Dakota enjoy the smells, but I also got a reminder from the elderly man to cherish my old dog every day. And I got to see, through witnessing Brad discover it, how much Dakota had changed over the years. He and I had both been too close to notice the subtle, day-to-day changes as they occurred, but since I was home with her all day, I was even closer. I experienced the tiny shifts alongside her: the decreased speed, the increased caution. It was fun to remember what she was like when she was younger, but I also loved who she'd become: my elder statesdog.

Beds and Priorities

P en in hand, I jotted down notes on a legal pad next to my laptop and external monitor. I had scheduled this particular meeting with my boss and one of my coworkers to discuss new ways to market our "Solar 101" webinars to a wider audience.

"The ads I've tested with the on-demand webinar haven't been very effective," I admitted, fearing how my boss might respond upon hearing that I had failed.

"Don't give up quite yet. You may just need more robust testing," he encouraged, his deep voice filling the room from my laptop speakers. "Could you share the results dashboard again?"

"Sure, one sec." I copied the document link and pasted it in the meeting chat bar. "It's in the chat."

As I listened to my boss's explanation of what he saw on the dashboard, a sound from the other side of my desk interrupted my concentration. It was Dakota shuffling against her bed or the rug, like she was struggling. I planted my feet on the floor and stood to see her squirming in her bed, trying to get her feet under her. On the white rug next to her bed was a dark smear. She'd had an accident while lying down, and now she couldn't get up.

In the chat window, I banged out a message as quickly as I could:

I'm so sorry! I have to go!

I didn't have time to explain. I closed my laptop and hurried to Dakota. Supporting her weight with my hands under her chest, I helped her to her feet. She had poop on her butt and one of her legs, and there was more on the rug. "You okay, puppy?" I rubbed her sides. "Yeah, you're okay. Let's go outside."

In the kitchen, I wet a few paper towels. Out back, I wiped off Dakota's fur and watched her amble around the backyard. As she peed, I stood there, holding the dirty paper towels. They were gross, but they were routine. Poop had been part of our lives for a while at this point.

When we came back inside, I threw the towels in the trash can, then grabbed the cleaning supplies off the counter without stopping and walked down the hall to my office. The odor had filled the room, and the concentrated smell hit me before I entered. "Hohhhh," I breathed out. I sucked in air through my lips while I cracked the window. I kneeled by the mess. I sprayed. I scrubbed. The poop had gotten on Dakota's bed, in addition to the rug. I sprayed again. Scrubbed again. Collected the soiled paper towels in a plastic grocery bag. Dakota lay behind me, supervising and waiting for access to her bed.

While cleaning up, I pondered what could be done about Dakota having such a hard time getting up from lying down. It was her dog beds that presented a problem; she did okay when getting up from lying on the carpet or one of the rugs, except for the living room rug, which was more slippery than the rest of them. We also had to switch out our coffee table for one she couldn't crawl underneath, after an incident when she scooted under it, lay down, and then couldn't stand back up. I didn't mind having rugs all over our hardwood floor but it was a bit of a bummer to take away her coffee table "den." She'd lie under there often, and she'd also use it as a "base" when Brad chased her around the house. She'd run from him and then dive underneath and Brad would pretend that it made her invisible, even though her head or tail would always stick out one end. "Dakota? Where are you?" Brad would ask, and she'd pop out like, "Here I am!"

Since I was home most of the time, I could help Dakota when she had trouble getting up out of her beds, but I wished I could prevent her from having to struggle with it at all—even for those few seconds while I ran over to assist. I hated to see her battle for something so basic to her well-being. I could fix long nails, clean up poop, and give her pain meds. But if she literally couldn't get up, I didn't know what I would do. Losing this ability—one of her last remaining pieces of autonomy and independence—wouldn't make for a good quality of life, and I knew it. I wondered if I could find or make a bed with taller sides that could act as barriers and keep her whole body inside the bed.

But right then, I needed to get back to work. I found an old towel in the hall closet and laid it on Dakota's bed so she wouldn't have to touch the wet spot. I also swiped a candle from the living room and lit it in my office to help cover the smell. After Dakota circled once and thumped down in her bed, I returned to my office chair and opened my laptop. The meeting had ended, so I messaged my boss:

> Shane, I'm so sorry for leaving the meeting without an explanation! My dog had an accident and needed some help, so I had to rush over there. I sincerely apologize. I hope we can continue the discussion we were having—or that you and Bill were able to.

I sat back in my chair for a moment. I didn't know Shane well enough yet to predict his answer, but I hoped that, even if he was angry, he would be kind in relaying that to me. I knew he might not appreciate witnessing his new employee choose her dog over her job at the drop of a hat (or a poop). I would do it again, though, so if he wanted an employee who prioritized work over loved ones, I knew I was going to continue disappointing him.

Three little dots appeared in the messaging platform. I braced myself for his response.

> Totally understand. Family comes first, and that includes your dog. We can schedule another meeting later in the week.

A smile came over my face as I read his words. This person who was supposed to care about my job performance above all else had not just let me off the hook for dropping work to help my dog, but he seemed to actually support and agree with my decision to do so. After leaving my animal advocacy job, I had worried that I would feel out of place back in "the real world," where not everybody feels like I do about animals. I worried I'd be the weird vegan, the annoying dog lady, the employee with priorities that were out of whack. But here was my new boss— who wasn't even a dog person—telling me it was okay for me to put Dakota first.

After work that evening, I circled back to the idea of finding a bed that would work better for Dakota. I held my hands above the keyboard and thought for several seconds. I tried a few search terms:

> dog bed with tall walls
> dog bed bumpers
> bed keep dog inside

After several failed searches, I opened Facebook and navigated to the Senior Dog Care Club group. I posted a question about the current predicament, along with a photo I'd taken of Dakota lying with her back end hanging off her bed.

In a matter of minutes, I had several responses to my post. Most were well meaning but not very helpful. A pug owner told me to buy a baby playpen. *My dog's got about thirty-five pounds on yours, dude, so a structure designed for a toddler ain't gonna cut it.* Someone else suggested I get a flat bed without any cushions around the edges. It sounded like it had worked for her dog, but Dakota did even worse in those types of beds. A few people told me to try CBD oil. There were always people in the group who swore—in all caps—that CBD solves everything.

Then a woman named Sarah, who had lost her dog, Phoebe, earlier that year, shared an idea that sounded like it could work. She recommended I use the bottom half of a large plastic dog crate. The sides on them are tall, and I could line it with blankets or even put a dog bed in it so Dakota would be both comfortable and safely secured. *Genius!*

That weekend, I went to the pet store and bought the biggest plastic dog crate they had. At home, I set aside the door and the screws and used the top and bottom parts to make two separate beds. I put a dog bed and blanket inside to make the new crate-bed soft. "Look, Dakota. Look, it's your new bed." She stared at me, uninterested in the bed but looking at me as if she were wondering if I had treats.

As I lay on the couch and turned the TV to an episode of *The Office*, Dakota stood nearby. "Lay down, pup," I told her. She did. She looked comfortable.

Later, Brad walked by on his way to the kitchen. "Check it out!" I told him. "A bucket bed."

"Nice work!"

I found it fulfilling to solve this kind of problem for Dakota. I was proud that I'd figured out a way to make her life better, a little easier, a little less painful. Of course, I wished she didn't have the problem to begin with, but if I could come up with a creative solution to solve it, or at least alleviate it, that made me feel useful.

That year, we didn't put up a Christmas tree. I don't remember why. I guess my focus was on taking care of Dakota and acclimating to my new job. Brad took a short trip to Illinois to visit his family over the holiday. Both of our moms had asked if I was coming along, since that was the first Christmas in five years that I didn't have to work on a big year-end fundraising campaign. In fact, at my new job, we got the entire week off between Christmas and New Year's.

Dakota couldn't travel, though, and I didn't want to leave her with anyone. So I stayed in Maryland, and she and I went to the dog park on Christmas Day, like we had the year before. I guess we were making our own little tradition.

Goodbye #8

Davey was a complicated dog with a complicated story. In the late 2000s, when Brad and I lived in North Carolina the second time, I did a lot to advocate for animals: started a vegetarian group; served on the board of directors for an animal shelter; penned a weekly newspaper column about animal rights and welfare issues; and joined an independent network of people throughout the state who helped homeless animals get adopted. That's how I met Davey. Somebody had rescued him from an animal control facility, a second person offered to transport him, and I volunteered to foster him until he could be adopted permanently.

Davey was a sturdy, seventy-pound, four-year-old hound dog with the dopiest eyes. His coat was black and brown, and a sideways *S* had been bleached into it on his right side, something hunters do to differentiate their dogs from other people's.

I think my house was the first one Davey had ever set foot in. He tried to climb onto my coffee table. The noise coming from the TV mesmerized him. He pawed at his water bowl until it spilled all over the floor. But he got along great with Dakota who was two at the time. They played together, sniffed around our yard together, and even napped by each other's sides in the sun's rays.

Still, fostering Davey presented some big challenges. He had come to live with us on a Saturday. Before I left for work the Monday after picking him up, I put him in Dakota's crate for the day. Since he wasn't neutered yet and we'd only known him for two days, I didn't trust him unsupervised with Dakota. I spread out a clear plastic drop cloth under the crate, just in case he peed while I was gone. He didn't, but he did reach through the bars of the crate, pull the plastic into the crate around all four sides, and chew it to shreds.

The next day, I tried him in the crate without a drop cloth. He literally chewed through the metal bars.

On day three, I tried leaving him in our fenced-in backyard. I figured he might do better there since he loved the outdoors and sunshine—and he certainly didn't seem to like being trapped in the house. I was wrong. He wedged his burly body through the three-inch gap at the bottom of our gate, and I had to leave work to pick him up after a neighbor called me, saying "I think I have your dog."

When it happened another time, I had no choice but to keep him inside. I trusted him with Dakota by then, but I knew I had to try to find him a family—quick! He tore up our house a little. Peed on things. Messed up the blinds. But luckily, nothing too serious.

I tried to train Davey to be a pet: to pee outside, to walk on a leash without breaking all the bones in my hand, to sit and stay. He successfully figured out sitting, but the rest was lost on him. He'd request attention from me by putting his paw on my leg when I was sitting on the couch. It would've been adorable if he had any grace, but his paw seemed to weigh as much as he did, and his claws would dig into my skin. As sweet as he was, and as well as he got along with Dakota, Davey was a very hard dog to love.

Several people took him to their homes for trial adoptions, but they always returned him, saying he wasn't quite right for them. I couldn't really blame them, but each "no" was a bigger disappointment than the previous one. Finally, I found Davey a family who was willing to accept him for who he was. But they left him in the backyard unsupervised, and he escaped.

They found him. He escaped again. Then a third time. They didn't know what to do with him, so I offered to take him back.

After eight months of fostering Davey and having no luck finding him a permanent home—or teaching him how to live in mine—I made the difficult decision to turn him over to the animal shelter where I served on the board. For me, surrendering an animal to a shelter was a cardinal sin. *You just don't do it,* I thought. *You find another way. You figure it out. You don't abandon the animal who counts on you.* Despite everything my heart was screaming at me, my brain knew he would be better off there. It was a no-kill shelter, and they'd be able to do a better job of keeping him safe and exposing him to potential adopters.

It worked. Not too long after I took Davey to the shelter, a great family adopted him. For safety and privacy reasons, they couldn't tell me who adopted him. While I was sad that I wouldn't be able to keep in touch with him or meet his new family, I was absolutely thrilled that he had one. Thrilled and relieved. That is, until I saw Davey's photo attached to a "lost dog" post on Craigslist.

After picking my jaw up off the floor, I responded to the post from Davey's new owner, explained who I was, and offered to help her find him. It turns out she had left him in the backyard for about three minutes as a test to see how her training with him was going, and he had jumped the fence.

We never did find Davey, and, to this day, I have no idea what happened to him. I like to pretend that the dog who didn't seem to fit in as a pet—that free-spirited, dopey boy—finally got his freedom. To think about it any other way is just too heartbreaking.

No Lasts Yet

Look at this." Brad stood next to me by the stove, holding
up his iPad.

When a video began playing, I thought, *Ugh.* I'm always
skeptical when someone wants to show me a video. It feels like
a chore.

My mind immediately flooded with questions. *What is this?
How long is it? Why is it so important that I watch it—and why right
now? Will it really be worth three minutes of my time?* When I saw
two baby pandas on the screen, more questions popped up: *Is
this a place that's using animals for entertainment? How were they
obtained? Are their needs being met? I don't like having to face the
reality that animals are so often viewed and used as commodities.
I'd rather not even see the video if that's the case.*

As I watched, I couldn't tell if it was a zoo or a sanctuary,
but I didn't see anything happening that I didn't like. The video
opened on a woman passing out bottles to panda cubs. I stood,
watching the screen, pushing bite-size pieces of vegan sausage
around a pan with a wooden spatula. Dakota lay nearby,

watching me cook and hoping I'd share my food. We joked that she was "watching her favorite show."

In the video, one of the panda cubs had trouble balancing his bottle, so the woman kept having to hold it steady for him. *I stand corrected*, I thought. *This is pretty entertaining.* "I like it." I smiled at Brad as the video ended.

"Yeah!" he said enthusiastically. He flipped the cover shut on his iPad and took a seat on the sunroom rug near Dakota but far enough away that she wouldn't get up and move. The girl does not like physical affection, especially while her show is on.

"We should get a baby panda." Brad said. He was pushing my buttons. I knew that and played along.

"No, we shouldn't," I scolded loudly. We both laughed.

Brad reopened his iPad and scrolled through Facebook for a minute. "When should we take Dakota to see snow?" he asked.

"I dunno," I said casually. I was open to suggestions but thought, *He should probably take the lead on this one.* We would both have to take vacation days, but at his job that was more difficult. The army has complicated procedures for everything, including asking for a day off. There's paperwork. Chain of command. And probably one of those big red stamps that say "APPROVED." At my job, I could just message my boss online and ask, "Is it cool if I don't come in on Friday?"

I continued pushing the sausage around, ready for Brad to toss out some dates that worked for him. When he didn't, I turned to see if he had gotten distracted. He hadn't. He was looking at me, his mind hard at work. We'd been living together for fifteen years, long enough for me to know what his facial expression meant. He was trying to find words that wouldn't hurt me and debating if he should say what he was thinking at all. "What?" I pressed him.

He relented, "This will probably be her last chance to see snow."

My thoughts raced. *What? No. You're wrong. She has more time than that. She's not even fifteen. She'll make it through another winter. You're saying she only has months? No. That's too soon. We have another year, at least. We're not doing "lasts" yet.*

I shifted my weight to the other leg and flipped the sausage pieces, which were browned on one side. Looking only at what I was doing and not at Brad, I set the spatula on the spoon rest next to the frying pan and turned to the fridge to get a soda. I was stalling. I didn't know what to say. I didn't know how to handle the situation. I wouldn't say I was sad or even mad. I was stubborn. Resistant. Defensive. I thought Brad was wrong, and yet I didn't want to say that. I didn't want to say *anything*. I wanted the conversation to be over. *We're gonna take Dakota to see snow, but not because it'll be her last chance. If he wants to think that, fine, but I know better.* I took a swig of soda and picked up the spatula again. "I'll ask around about where we can go," I said.

That night, after brushing my teeth, changing into pajamas, and administering pills, I lay with Dakota in her bed on our bedroom floor. It sat between our two closets in a nook that was three feet wide, slightly larger than the bed itself. Since there were walls on either side of the bed, we could keep a regular dog bed in there rather than needing a bucket bed.

I lay on my side, propped up on an elbow, my head leaning on the palm of my hand. I was aware that I'd get dog hair all over my T-shirt and pajama pants just before getting into my own bed, but I was okay with that.

Dakota was curled up in a ball next to me. I pet her softly, more for me than for her. I traced the contours of her face with my fingers. She closed her eyes as I gripped and massaged the loose skin on the back of her neck. "What do you need all that skin for?" I asked playfully.

I gently ran my hand over her side, feeling her rib cage underneath my palm. "You're such a good girl," I said softly. Again, more for me than for her.

I kissed Dakota between the eyes, which she opened to a squint to see what I was doing. Then she pulled her front legs in toward her body and drifted off to sleep. I closed my eyes too and continued petting her, reflecting on what Brad had said earlier and how I'd taken it.

I shouldn't have been surprised to learn that he had a prediction about Dakota's life span. He was constantly thinking—worrying—about the future. He tries to predict it so he can prepare for any possible negative scenario. Not me. I live happily in my ignorance. Of course, I thought all the time about losing Dakota one day, about how painful that would be when the time came. I dreaded it, but I didn't think in specifics. I hadn't given any thought to our daily activities being Dakota's lasts. My view of the situation was cropped, and the bad stuff was outside the frame. My brain was very proficient at protecting me from pain.

Hearing that Brad had a prediction at all was jarring enough. But adding the fact that it was a much shorter timeline than I would've guessed felt like my heart had been punched in the face. You know, if hearts had faces. I hadn't entertained the idea of losing Dakota that year. I'd always hoped she would live a long life. And by "long," I mean very, *very* long. She was always so healthy, and even with her mobility issues, she still got around better and looked better off than most dogs I saw her age—and even younger. At fourteen and a half, she had already lived a long time for a dog her size. I knew that intellectually, but that all went out the window when we were talking about my Dakota. She had to live longer because she was exceptional and because losing her was unimaginable. She was my everything.

My mind jumped back to Dakota's first snowfall. It was 2009, and she was four years old. She'd only lived in North Carolina and California at that point, so although she'd seen snow on road trips, she'd never actually romped or played in it. One Tuesday morning, as I was getting ready to leave for work, my cell phone rang.

"Nobody should be out driving in this," the voice said sweetly yet matter-of-factly. It was our human resources director calling to say she'd decided to close the office for the day. I was surprised. I'd heard North Carolinians aren't used to snow, but there was only supposed to be a couple of inches on the ground that day.

I'm a midwesterner, and I'm also not a fan of being told what to do. So, typically, someone's insistence that I shouldn't drive to work in two inches of snow would annoy me. But this particular day happened to be January 20, the day of President Obama's first inauguration. I was thrilled to have an excuse to stay home and watch the ceremony on TV. I had volunteered for the campaign a handful of times and was inspired by our new president. I'm not someone who feels patriotic often, but seeing the first Black man elected president did the trick. I would've been bummed to miss his inauguration. Getting to see Dakota play in the snow for the first time would be icing on the cake.

"Oh, okay," I said into the phone politely. I thanked her, hung up, and celebrated my day off. After bundling up, I opened the back door. Dakota trotted out onto the deck, sniffed the ground, and then proceeded to have the time of her life. She sniffed all around excitedly. She followed her nose to the middle of the yard, stopped, turned to the side, then ran after an invisible enemy, keeping her body low to the ground. She pounced on the snow and sniffed at it again. I giggled, amused by her antics. She scooped up some of the dust with her mouth and swallowed it, leaving some white dust on her muzzle. I snapped a few photos to show Brad, who was in Iraq at the time. Later, I'd joked with him via email about giving Dakota cocaine.

After ten minutes of watching Dakota play in the snow, I went inside and got an old towel to place on the floor by the back door. Then I let Dakota inside, wiped the snow from between her paw pads and off her nose, and towel dried her body so she wouldn't be cold. She stood there patiently, lifting each leg so I could clean it. Once dry, I released her with an "Okay," and she shook off and pranced into the living room, satisfied with her play session.

She spent the rest of the morning curled up in her bed next to the couch while I watched the inauguration. "On this day, we gather because we have chosen hope over fear . . . ," Obama preached.

Back in our bedroom, as I lay with Dakota in her bed, I realized why I'd reacted so poorly to Brad's comment in the kitchen. I'd been letting my fears determine my hopes, and those hopes had solidified into expectations. I expected Dakota to live longer than other dogs just because I *loved* her more. I was in denial. I saw it clearly then. I'd progressed from denying that Dakota was getting old, to trying to prevent it, to finding fixes for all the little issues brought on by her aging. I put down rugs, cleaned up poop, trimmed her nails, created bucket beds. I even found a new job that caused me less stress and I could still do from home so I could be with her. I was fixing everything. But I was also avoiding the reality that losing her was inevitable.

I could still hope that we would have another year together, another winter. But I needed to come to terms with the reality that, one day, I would have to say goodbye.

Snow Trip

The smell hit my nostrils as we pulled into the hotel parking lot. "Did she poop?"

Brad looked in the back seat. "Yeeeah, she did," he said, drawing out the vowels with a sympathetic tone. *Well, a vacation with an elderly dog isn't gonna come without some hiccups,* I thought.

He headed into the lobby to check us in and get our room key. I lifted Dakota out of the big dog bed in our back seat, where she'd been lying and where she'd had the accident. I set her down on the snow-covered asphalt, doing my best to avoid the icy spots. She stood by, smelling the unfamiliar air while she waited to see what came next.

I started cleaning up the mess and tending to her at the same time, a familiar process at this point. Holding the leash with my right hand, I used my left to get out the cleaning products stashed in my car.

I put one hand under Dakota's belly to support her weight, and, with the other, I used the paper towels to wipe the little bit of poop off her leg. I put the soiled paper towels in a plastic bag, which flapped around in the wind, making what should've been a simple task more difficult. My eyes watered from the cold, and I felt my hands tensing up quickly without any winter gloves on. If I'd put them on though, I knew the task would take even longer *and* I'd risk getting poop on them.

I turned my head to check on Dakota, who was standing at the end of the leash, her back legs starting to buckle.

"I know, puppy," I said reassuringly. Using the plastic bag, I picked up the poop in the back seat as quickly as I could. Then I left both rear car doors open to air it out and carefully walked Dakota around the front of the car to the snow-covered grass. "Let's go pee."

After she sniffed the grass and peed, I let her walk around some more since her back legs were more stable when she was moving. I glanced toward the front door of the hotel, hoping Brad would come out soon.

A minute later, he came bounding across the parking lot to the car. He was excited to get back to us, plus he was freezing.

"She peed," I reported. "Wanna walk her around and I'll finish cleaning her bed?"

As he slowly walked her around the grass, I glanced over frequently. He made a snowball and tossed it in the air for Dakota to catch, but she didn't play along. "I think she's too cold to play right now," he said. We decided to get settled in our hotel room and take a break from the cold, then come back out later that afternoon.

Our hotel room was decorated like a cabin, with big vaulted wood ceilings and a brick fireplace. Dakota and I went in first, bringing one of her beds and a towel with us. Brad started bringing in the rest of our stuff: two suitcases; food and water bowls; a container of dog food; and a tote bag filled with treats, a Kong, a jar of peanut butter, a butter knife, and Dakota's medicines.

"Uh-oh," I groaned when I entered. In the pictures I'd seen online, the room was carpeted. This one had hardwood floors.

I set down Dakota's bed and laid the towel out as a partial pathway for her to walk on. When Brad came in with the rest of our stuff, we put down another bed and towel. I got out the Kong, peanut butter, and knife and prepared a treat for Dakota. She lowered her body onto one of the beds, wedging the Kong between it and a nearby piece of furniture to keep it still while she licked the peanut butter from it. I watched her in case she ended up in any weird positions or with her hind end on the slippery floor.

Other than the hardwood, the hotel room was great, as was the whole area: Deep Creek Lake in Maryland. It met my criteria for our old-dog-cation: it had enough snow on the ground for Dakota to romp in and was within 250 miles of Walter Reed. Any farther than that and Brad would've had to take official leave, the army's term for vacation. For some reason, the army feels the need to have its own terms for concepts there are already words for.

Before settling on Deep Creek Lake, I had asked my coworkers for recommendations of locations with guaranteed snow. One person suggested a ski resort in Pennsylvania, which sounded great because if there wasn't adequate snow, they'd dump fake snow on the ground. Plus, it sounded cozy, like there would be cabins and fireplaces and hot cocoa. I couldn't tell from their website if dogs were allowed in the lodge, so, brave millennial that I am, I called them on the phone.

I didn't realize until I was talking with the receptionist that I'd entered uncharted territory—for me and probably for the young-sounding woman on the phone. I was going to say out loud for the first time why we were taking this trip. "We're thinking of visiting to let our dog enjoy the snow. She's almost fifteen." I had typed those words to my coworkers on Slack when asking for recommendations, but the sounds hadn't left my mouth until that phone call with a stranger. I don't know how I was able to keep my voice from cracking.

I can't remember if I actually needed to share with her the reason for our trip. I think I was just trying to convey to her that we wouldn't bother anyone. Dakota wouldn't be running around disturbing the snow or being loud or pooping everywhere. We just wanted to bring our old, sweet dog to walk around and catch a few gently tossed snowballs. But dogs weren't allowed there, so I thanked her and moved on.

Another coworker had suggested Deep Creek Lake after a recent visit with his family. I looked online for hotels near the lake and found this inn, which seemed perfect. It has first-floor rooms, fireplaces, plenty of space outside to walk around, and the lake is just a one-minute walk across the parking lot.

After we warmed up and Dakota finished her Kong, we were ready to head back outside. Brad grabbed the dog coat he'd borrowed from a colleague, who had a golden retriever. The coat was red plaid at the top, black at the bottom, and had white trim. "We're gonna get blonde dog hair all over the black cloth," I had told Brad when I first saw it the night before our trip.

"Evan won't mind," he'd assured me.

We handled Dakota gingerly, putting her left leg in first, straightening out the coat across her back, then doing the right leg. We put on our own coats, which was much easier, then our hats and gloves, and headed outside.

Our hotel room was on the back side of the inn, facing out onto a deck. With a ramp next to the set of stairs outside our room, it was like this place was tailor-made for us. We walked down the ramp to the snow-covered grass, then Brad took Dakota around to sniff and romp in the snow. She moved slowly, carefully, but the expression on her face made it obvious that she was enjoying herself. Her nose wiggled, taking in all the novel scents, and her ears perked up, listening for new sounds. Watching her filled me with joy. I started to think about this potentially being her last time in the snow, but I pushed the thought out of my mind. It wasn't the time for sadness. This trip was all about joy.

Brad let Dakota lead, keeping the leash loose and walking in whichever direction she chose. It was a game we'd played with her since she was little.

"Which way?" Brad asked. Dakota followed her nose to the right. "Okay, good decision." He walked beside her, holding the leash high in the air so it wouldn't get tangled under her legs while she was walking close to him.

About ten minutes later, Dakota's back legs started to buckle, and we didn't want to overdo it with the cold weather, so we went back inside for the evening.

After a quick Google search to find a restaurant nearby, I ordered food for the three of us and left to pick it up from down the street. When I returned, Brad ran to the hotel lobby and brought back two logs for the fireplace. It was cold in our room despite the heat being on. He started a fire, and I put one of Dakota's beds and a bowl of rice and broccoli by the fireplace. Brad and I watched, grinning, as she stood eating it and then licked the bowl across the floor. I stepped in to hold it still for her so she could finish her meal. Brad gave her a few bites of his pizza as a dessert. She devoured all of it.

When it was time to go to sleep, I put Dakota's big oval bed by the fire so she could lie in front of it. Then I laid her other bed next to it so if her butt hung off the main one, it would still land on a soft surface instead of the floor.

Dakota lay down, and Brad and I got in our bed nearby. But I struggled to get comfortable or fall asleep. The heat still wasn't kicking in, and we were all cold. I got up and put on a thick pair of socks and a sweatshirt, then placed a big towel on Dakota and rubbed her side gently to warm her. Brad added the second log to the fire.

I worried about Dakota being cold. The trip was supposed to be full of positive experiences for her, and I didn't want her to be uncomfortable. I wanted her to sleep soundly by a fire and have pleasant dreams and get some good rest before the fun we'd have in the snow the next day. If the room didn't get warmer, I didn't know what we'd do. Worst case scenario, we might've had to cut the trip short. I wanted everything to go smoothly and for the trip to be a positive experience for her and for us. I was acutely aware that we were making memories.

I considered putting Dakota on our bed so she'd be able to soak up our body heat. Who was I kidding—Brad's body heat. But I reconsidered because I knew if she were to jump down while we were asleep, she would hurt herself. Luckily, the fire got going and the heat finally kicked in, warming up the room to a toasty, comfortable temperature. I snuck a picture of Dakota soundly sleeping all cozy by the fire.

The next morning, we showered and packed our things. For breakfast, we ate leftovers from dinner. We walked around outside the inn, letting Dakota smell whatever she wanted to. We crossed the parking lot to look at the lake and take a few pictures in front of it. Dakota stood for them with her back legs bent slightly, a reminder of her muscle weakness. As we walked back across the parking lot, we noticed Dakota's legs still buckling. They usually only did that when she was standing still. We figured that meant she was cold and maybe feeling weak, so we took a break in our hotel room.

These short trips outside and frequent breaks weren't disappointing for us, nor were they surprising. We'd gone there knowing Dakota's physical limitations. And the trip was for her. Whatever she could handle, whatever she wanted to do, that's what we were there to do.

As we warmed up inside, Brad and I made plans for what to do next. We decided to visit a nearby dog park and then head home to Silver Spring.

We were the only people at the park—maybe because it was cold and snow-covered, or maybe because it was a Sunday morning in a rural area and everyone was at church. Whatever the reason, it was nice to have the park to ourselves. I walked Dakota through the gate and removed her leash. She walked around, not far from us, smelling the ground, the fence, and the legs of the picnic benches. Brad jogged to the far side of the park and called Dakota. She trotted over to him slowly, stopping a few times to sniff irresistible smells on the ground. Brad formed snowballs in his hands and tossed them to her. Some she missed and others she caught in her mouth, eating a few and causing the rest to break apart upon impact with her snout. As I watched them play together, I thought about how grateful I was feeling. I knew this was exactly what Brad had hoped to get out of the trip—not just to see Dakota enjoy herself but to be the cause of that enjoyment. I took pictures and videos to capture the moment.

Walking back toward the gate, I went slowly, and Dakota walked alongside me. I felt a special connection when walking with her, especially without a leash. We only ever let Dakota off leash if we knew it was safe, like at dog beaches in California (sorry, babies), fenced-in dog parks, and one time on a country road in Tennessee.

When my grandpa died in 2018, I'd taken Dakota with me to the Volunteer State for his funeral. I'd felt awkward and sad for much of the trip, but I treasured my stroll with Dakota down my aunt's driveway the day after my grandpa's funeral. Dakota and I had ventured out to get some air and visit the two horses down the street. On our way back, the lure of country living overcame me and I got the urge to remove Dakota's leash. I tossed the handle over her back, and she walked beside me, attached to me only by habit, not nylon.

We walked in silence, except for the sound of wind, my light breathing, and a little panting by Dakota. There was nothing going on around us. No hustle, no bustle. I told Brad later that I could see myself living in the country, walking on our land in the mornings and evenings, enjoying the fresh air, and letting Dakota walk freely. He'd responded, "I'm gonna hold you to it."

Walking with Dakota at the snowy dog park reminded me of that walk in Tennessee. She'd declined a lot since then, lost a lot of muscle mass, and couldn't go on that long of a road trip anymore. Even this three-hour drive had been a lot for her. Brad told me he could identify her footprints because of the strips of missing snow behind them from her dragging her back feet. But she was still happy. Still walking. Still wiggling her nose at the air.

On our drive back home, I reflected on the trip. It was exactly what I'd wanted. It was a chance to be together, to be present, to enjoy Dakota, and to give her all the joyful and fun experiences we could. And that's what we did.

When we stopped at a rest area to let Dakota pee and stretch her legs, there was a section of grass with a picnic table on it. But a sign with a stick figure image of a dog with a line through it made it clear that we weren't welcome there.

Dakota and I posed for a picture by it because we were rebels and we were full of life.

A week and a half after we returned home, the governor announced a state of emergency in Maryland. The first cases of COVID-19 had been diagnosed in the United States, and all businesses deemed unessential were shut down. Had we waited even two more weeks, we wouldn't have been able to take our trip with Dakota.

Brad had to cancel all his patients' nonemergency appointments and work from home for six weeks. He studied, worked on PowerPoint slides for virtual presentations, and got some much-needed downtime in between. My job didn't change much since I already worked from home. The main sacrifice I had to make due to COVID was trying to appear patient with colleagues who were new to virtual meetings and could never figure out whether they were on mute.

The shutdown started in March and was only supposed to last a few weeks, but as we all now know, it went on for much longer. As the weather grew warmer, I started getting together with friends for outdoor activities. We met up for hikes and backyard happy hours. We attended the occasional protest to support the Black Lives Matter movement, which experienced a resurgence at the same time as the pandemic. Other than those few outings, I was okay with staying home. I didn't particularly like leaving Dakota anyway.

Behind the Shed

Spring meant Dakota and I could spend more time in our backyard, and we each had our routines. Hers was to walk the perimeter counterclockwise, scanning the ground near the fence along the right side of the yard first, then underneath the trees by the back fence, and, finally, behind the shed. Mine was to sit on the step of the deck, scrolling through social media and checking email.

One day in May, I looked up from my phone to see an empty yard. *Behind the shed*, I thought.

That was Dakota's favorite place to forage for forbidden foods, and her "food brain" had vastly intensified in her old age. She'd find nuts that squirrels had dropped as they scrambled through the fir trees overhead. She'd sniff out droppings from the mice that had ventured up from the nearby woods at night. She even ate dirt sometimes. She'd eat anything remotely edible. Once in a while, she'd luck out and find a "treat" that one of the neighbor's outdoor cats had deposited on the ground the previous night. As the saying goes, one cat's poop is another dog's breakfast.

"Dakota, c'mere!" I sang in a cheerful tone. Our yard wasn't huge, but it had a few hiding spots where she'd go to eat things she shouldn't.

She didn't come.

"Dakota, come here!" I tried again in a deeper voice.

Still nothing.

Usually, she'd come trotting over upon hearing that deeper tone. I labeled it my "man voice" and joked with Brad that Dakota was sexist because it was the only time she heard me. But even that wasn't working this time. Our backyard was an all-you-can-eat buffet for Dakota, so it was harder to get her attention out there.

Amused at the situation, I stood up and put my phone in my back pocket, then walked diagonally across the yard toward the shed. I smiled as I thought about the plan to catch her in the act of eating something she shouldn't be.

I took careful steps, sneaking around the side of the shed. *When I see her, I'll throw my arms up, hop, and exclaim, "What are you doing?!" Then I'll tussle the fur on the back of her neck, and we'll go back inside for a treat.* It was a delightful plan.

I rounded the corner of the shed. *Oh my God.*

Dakota was lying on her belly with all four legs splayed out in one direction and her eyes looking up at me. I rushed over and lifted her to her feet. "You okay, puppy?" I asked, rubbing her side.

I stood there for a moment, hunched over and hugging her torso, stunned by sadness and guilt and sympathy. I wondered how long she'd been lying there helpless, waiting for me to come rescue her. *Had she tried to get up? Was she in any pain, either from falling or from lying with her legs splayed out for that period of time? Had she wondered why I wasn't coming over to help her? What did she imagine I was doing that was more important? Why hadn't I gone with her instead of staring at my stupid phone?*

"I'm so sorry," I said, my face buried in Dakota's scruffy fur.

When I let go of her, I watched her every move as she took a few steps forward. She lowered her head toward the ground, sniffed, and ate a piece of dirt—like nothing had happened.

After that, I almost always accompanied Dakota when she went outside. There was one other time I didn't. I think I was just being lazy. From the sunroom, I watched her through the window as she squatted to pee and fell backward onto her butt. I slipped on Brad's shoes and sprinted out to help her up. She wasn't hurt—or even affected, really—but the sight of it is still seared into my memory, and it's almost as awful to recall as it was to live through. Dakota, sitting on her butt, legs splayed forward. Waiting. Unable to do anything until someone came to her rescue.

It seemed like every time I got comfortable or complacent, something else would surprise me and rob Dakota of a little more independence. I was there, willing to help with everything, but looking back, I know it took a toll on me.

Goodbye #9

It's hard for me to think about Callie. I met her about a year after the Davey situation. Her family was dealing with a sick parent in another state, and they weren't able to give her the attention she deserved. I thought Dakota, who was nearly three years old then, would enjoy having a playmate. When I saw the Craigslist post about Callie needing a new home, I drove an hour to Raleigh to pick her up for a trial adoption.

Callie was black, lanky like Dakota but slightly smaller. She and Dakota got along fairly well, although Callie was a bit dominant and played rougher than Dakota—and nonstop. The rambunctiousness of two dogs together made me feel overwhelmed, and I didn't love that Callie asserted dominance over Dakota, even though Dakota was a good sport about it.

As I drove Callie back to her original family, the whole way I thought about how I shouldn't have taken her in—even for a trial run. I should've put more thought into what it might be like to have two dogs. I should've been positive that's what I wanted before trying to add a second dog to our family. I had

given her a new home and then changed my mind. I had gotten her family's hopes up. And, worst of all, I had broken my promise to myself about what kind of person I was: someone who would never abandon her dog.

Team Dakota

Wanna go see the cherry blossoms this weekend?" Brad asked, looking up from his iPad. I lay on the love seat, scrolling through Facebook on my phone. We were both half watching a rerun of *Parks and Recreation*.

I thought about telling him no—that I didn't want to bring Dakota because she didn't do well in the car anymore, but I didn't want to leave her either. But we also couldn't do many fun activities together thanks to the shutdown, and I figured Dakota would be okay for a few hours. She would just sleep.

"Sure, I—"

Before I could finish, Brad jumped up from the couch and ran over to Dakota. I looked up, concerned. The base of her tail was moving up and down. Tail pumping. She was about to poop.

My concern shifted from wondering what was wrong to anticipating how Brad would handle it. I watched nervously, trying not to interfere.

Brad stood Dakota up and led her toward the back door. "Come on, come on, come on!"

Dakota couldn't move quickly, so she was pooping well before they got outside. In the dining room. In the sunroom. By the time they got to the back door, she was done. "Go outside," he instructed her.

"She doesn't need to now," I chimed in from the love seat. I couldn't help myself. I'd told him several times before that trying to rush her only made things worse. I was annoyed that he'd made Dakota go outside by herself when she didn't even need to do anything out there. *Does he really think she isn't done pooping? Is he trying to punish her or teach her a lesson for something she didn't do on purpose?* I couldn't come up with a reason I didn't dislike.

That wasn't the first time Dakota pooping inside had frustrated Brad. He didn't agree that we should let her do it, so he insisted on trying to prevent it from happening. I had tried that too—at first. But I found that it always ended in more of a mess. When you try to rush an elderly dog while she's pooping, her poops just go rogue and roll away. Then, not only do you have to clean up poop, you also have to find it first. It's like a treasure hunt that nobody wants to be on.

Working from home made things a little easier. I could take her out proactively. We went out every time I needed a break from work and anytime I got up to make lunch or grab a soda from the fridge. All our activities were punctuated by a trip outside. It was kind of like we'd reverted to our house-training days when Dakota was a puppy in that North Carolina apartment.

Back then, I'd put Dakota in her crate for a nap, and when it was time to let her out, we'd go outside right away so she could pee. We'd come back inside, play for a bit, and then go outside again. Come back in to eat, go outside again. It didn't take long for her to get used to going out when she needed to pee or poop. And while it might sound like a pain to take her out so often, that's what's required to house-train a dog. Plus, I wasn't working, so I had all day to help her learn.

But with Dakota's advanced age, she wasn't able to hold her bowels or let me know when she needed to go out. *She* didn't know. I took her out a lot, but it wasn't a foolproof solution.

So my philosophy was to let it be. To accept it and try not to make it worse. Whenever I noticed Dakota's tail pumping, I'd go help her out of bed and support her weight with my hand under her belly or behind her thigh so she didn't slip on our thin living room rug. I'd stand there, crouched over her, while she pooped inside. Brad saw it as me letting her do something she shouldn't. I saw it as making the inevitable mess a little less messy. With my method, all the poop came out in one place, so the cleanup was easier.

Sure, it was gross. I did a good job cleaning it, but all our rugs were surely covered in poop cooties. I knew we'd be trashing them before our next move when Brad finished his residency program. I didn't care. As the saying goes, "Shit happens." Sometimes it happens on a rug. *Big whoop,* I thought. *Rugs are replaceable.* Upset with Brad, I stayed put on the love seat and left him to clean up the poop.

Brad had always been my partner in caring for and loving Dakota. He shared my convictions about doing whatever was best for her and my hopes that she would live the best life possible for as long as possible. He was never annoyed to have to take her to the vet or give her medicine or spend thousands of dollars on her care. If he was, he never let it show. So when Dakota's accident upset him, it shook me. It made me feel like, in that instance, we were no longer on the same team. And if I had to choose, I was picking Team Dakota.

I didn't take too kindly to anyone acting like or implying that taking care of Dakota was a bother or a stressor. I guess it was all part of my denial. I'd finally come to terms with Dakota being old, and I was even starting to accept that she wouldn't live forever. But this new version of denial had me refusing to acknowledge or admit that taking care of her in her old age could ever be burdensome.

At the time, it didn't bother me that I had to clean up poop or put rugs all over the house. Looking back, I can see that it actually *was* difficult. Not the messes, necessarily, but what they represented. Caring for Dakota in her old age—watching her decline—came with an awareness that we were nearing the end of her life. I didn't know when it would come, but I knew we were heading toward it. That knowledge was a heavy weight to bear. On top of that, my new job was beginning to shift toward being stressful. My boss did his best to shield me from taking on too much, but I started to feel a hint of that familiar feeling from my previous job. I was getting overwhelmed. Luckily, since this job wasn't my passion, I could treat it more like a job and at least unplug every evening and on the weekends.

A few days after the accident that frustrated Brad, Dakota peed on the living room rug. I reacted calmly and I didn't try to stop her because I knew it was too late. While she'd had full control of her bladder until then, she'd been unable to control her bowels for over a year. I was used to seeing new issues pop up for her as she aged, and this felt like a typical one—not one I had expected, but not one that shocked me either.

"That's okay, puppy." I spoke to Dakota but was consoling myself as well. I ambled into the kitchen, grabbed the rug cleaning supplies that had taken up permanent residence on the counter, and cleaned up the spot on our rug.

That evening, I told Brad what had happened.

"What are we gonna do?" he asked with urgency.

"I don't know," I responded defensively.

"Pee isn't like poop. It's gonna ruin the floors."

"I know," I said, as if it was something I'd thought of before he said it. I hadn't. But he had a point. We'd be moving in a year and would need to sell or rent out our house, and it couldn't have urine-soaked floors.

I already knew about doggy diapers from the senior dog Facebook group, so I ordered a pack of three. I'd seen other senior dog caretakers recommend Poise pads for incontinence, so I bought two packs of those too. The pads would go inside the diapers for better absorption.

When the diapers arrived two days later, I opened them right away. Dakota hadn't peed inside since that first time, so I didn't think she needed to wear the diapers yet, but I wanted to make sure they fit. The set I had chosen came with three colors: black, hot pink, and lavender. Pink felt too girly, and black would immediately look filthy when Dakota's blonde fur shed all over it, so I pulled out the lavender diaper and unlatched the sides.

"Dakota, c'mere." She strolled over, unsuspecting. "Look at this." I let her smell the diaper before I tried it on her. She stood, a little wobbly but accommodating.

One end of the diaper had a small hole for Dakota's tail to go through. I reached my fingers in and guided her tail through it. She looked back at me with some major side-eye. "Oh, good girl, Peepers. I know, this is ridiculous."

Her legs began bending under her weight, so I let her take a couple of steps forward before I wrapped the diaper around her hind end and latched the sides. I stepped back and took her picture. She looked pitiful. The diaper covered her back end but sat below her waist, and her barrel chest made it look even smaller.

"Okay. Good girl," I told her and took off the diaper. *It'll do.*

Later that day, the Poise pads arrived on our front porch, and I realized I'd made two mistakes when ordering them. Not only did I accidentally purchase the extralong ones, but I also didn't check to see how many came in a pack. Since I'd ordered two packs, I ended up with a stash of 180 enormous pads in my guest room. *Well, at least we're prepared.*

Overthinking

It turns out that staying at home during a pandemic provides you with abundant free time. To read. To research. To think. Perhaps to overthink.

As the caretaker for an elderly dog, I had something concrete and terrifying to overthink about. *How will I know when it's time? How will I handle that? What will it look like? What will it feel like? What if I refuse to face it? Will Brad have to shake me and talk some sense into me?*

One Thursday evening after an overthinking session, I pushed off the floor with my feet and rolled my office chair away from my desk. I stood. I walked. Before I knew it, I was standing at the top of the stairs leading to the basement. I didn't need to prop up the baby gate anymore because Dakota just stayed off the stairs at this point. I'm not sure if it was out of habit or if she knew she shouldn't use them. I took a deep breath in and exhaled as I walked down the steps.

When I rounded the corner at the bottom of the stairs, Brad was sitting on the left side of the futon, leaning against a stack of cushions and holding a video game controller with both hands. I sat down cross-legged on the floor to his left. When we made eye contact, he placed his hand on his headphones.

"Hey, one sec," he said into the microphone and pressed a button to mute himself.

"What's up?" he said to me as he took off the headphones and set them off to his right.

I stalled. I needed to figure out how to say this. And how to avoid crying once I started to speak.

For the past twenty minutes, I'd been upstairs reading about in-home euthanasia on the Lap of Love website. I read about the process: how you set up an appointment, what you need to do to prepare, and then what happens during the procedure. I read advice articles that suggested it's better to be too early than "too late," when your dog is already in tremendous pain and unable to pass away comfortably or peacefully.

"I was reading on this website," I continued. "You know Lap of Love?" Brad nodded. "I'm wondering if I should call them and give them our contact and credit card info now, for when the time comes."

"Sure?" He said it as a question but in a way I took to be supportive yet curious about the reasoning behind my idea.

I didn't think the day was coming soon, but ever since Brad had mentioned Dakota's "lasts," I realized and could admit that it was coming at some point. And I knew I wanted it to happen at home, especially since the pandemic meant we weren't allowed to go into vet clinics. There was no way I was ever going to drop her off and wait in the car.

I told Brad I was worried that in the midst of horrible sadness I'd have to do administrative things like read my credit card to someone over the phone. Since I didn't know how to prepare for the emotional fallout that day would bring—or even want to think about it—I focused instead on the logistics. Figuring out who we would call and how much it would cost was way easier than facing the thought of how much it was going to hurt.

Witnessing a loved one get older is full of vulnerability. Feelings made me uncomfortable—my own and other people's too. When my friends or family members felt sad, I'd say something awkward and robotic like, "I'm sorry you're sad," and I'd tell them to call me if they wanted someone to tell jokes and lighten the mood. That's the role I could fill and the type of support I was comfortable providing.

I didn't like it when people were sad in front of me, and I didn't like being sad in front of them.

Research professor and best-selling author Brené Brown says that vulnerability is necessary if you want to live a fullhearted life. As a shame researcher, she found that you can't have courage without vulnerability. You also can't have all kinds of other cool things, like creativity, innovation, or connection. In her first TED Talk, Brené admitted to being bummed when she discovered that vulnerability is so important. I, too, was annoyed when I learned it from her.

Brené's 2019 Netflix special, *The Call to Courage*, came out when Dakota was nearing fourteen. I watched it right away, not thinking about applying any of what I learned to my role as Dakota's person. But as Dakota continued to age, I began to see its relevance. In the special, Brené says that 95 percent of parents do what she calls "dress rehearsing tragedy." When they feel an immense amount of love and the vulnerability that comes with it, their minds immediately jump to worst-case scenarios, like baby snatchings and car accidents.

I'm very familiar with this concept because my mom has done it since I was born. Even now that I'm an adult, she asks if my doors are locked, recommends that I avoid certain areas while traveling, and has nightmares about me drowning or being snatched by abductors. It doesn't help that she consumes the most horrifying media available, like *Law & Order: SVU* and the local evening news. I asked her once what podcasts she listens to, and this was the list:

Forensic Files
Crimes of Passion
Dateline
Park Predators
Crime Junkies
Locked Up Abroad
Motive for Murder
I Survived
Happiness Lab

Yeah, that last one intrigued me too.

I guess I should be grateful that my mom loves me enough to imagine horrible things happening to me all the time. But following Brené's advice seems like a more pleasant way to deal with all that love. She recommends identifying those moments when you begin dress rehearsing tragedy and using them as reminders to practice gratitude instead.

I did that with Dakota. I often found myself feeling sad that she'd be gone one day. She'd be curled up in her bed and I'd experience my thoughts go from love to fear of losing her. I'd notice this shift and remind myself to focus on feeling grateful. Thinking about the future without Dakota meant that my mind was somewhere else. By being grateful, I was present. And she deserved that from me, especially if her time was limited.

It's easier said than done, though, and I wasn't always good at it, but I got pretty consistent. I would lie with Dakota in her bed on our bedroom floor, just petting and looking at her.

"I love you so much," I'd say. "You're my best friend in the whole world." Apparently, being vulnerable turns me into a five-year-old child.

"I'm so glad I've gotten to spend so many years with you," I'd whisper to her while stroking the scruffy, loose fur on her neck.

If she could've spoken English, I'm sure she would've said "stop crowding me"—exactly what I tell my mom.

Back in the basement that day when I'd brought up Lap of Love, Brad pointed out that, when the time came, I wouldn't be alone. He'd be there with me, able to help with anything that needed to be done. I wouldn't have to deal with the heartbreak and also handle all the logistics. We'd be a team. In fact, both of us had always assumed that Brad would take care of most of it— that he'd be the stable one and I'd be a train wreck. Those are the roles we usually assume when facing serious problems. And I knew this would be the biggest, most serious heartbreak I'd ever faced. I had no real understanding of how it would feel to lose Dakota, but I knew it would be incapacitating. "You'll have to hide all our knives because I'm gonna try to go with her," I'd joke to Brad.

We discussed it for several minutes, being mindful of the words we used—and didn't use: *when it's time* instead of *when she dies* and *process* in place of *euthanasia*.

We decided it'd be a good idea for me to email Lap of Love in advance, so I sent the following:

> May 28, 2020
> 7:06 p.m.
> To: Lap of Love
>
> Good evening,
>
> First, I want to thank you for this incredible service you provide. I'm so glad you exist.
>
> We're not ready for your in-home euthanasia service yet, but we're nearing that time. I want to check in with you on a few things:
>
> - Are you still providing in-home euthanasia during COVID?
> - Do you come out to Silver Spring?
> - Is it okay to give you my information now, hopefully at least a couple months before we'll need to use your service? I know I'll be a wreck when the time comes, and it'd be nice to get the "business" parts out of the way ahead of time.
>
> Thank you very much,
> Lisa

The Train

It was Wednesday, June 3, and work was hectic. With four meetings on my calendar, it was going to be almost impossible to check any actual tasks off my to-do list. If I did, they'd just be replaced with new ones, like that assembly line scene at a candy factory in *I Love Lucy*. Sure, I could hide the unfinished tasks in my hat like Lucy and Ethel did, but then my boss, thinking I could handle even more work, would yell to the conveyor belt operator to "speed it up a little," and I'd be even more screwed.

I survived three of the four meetings that should've been emails and had just one more Zoom call to go. I knew this last call would be a series of updates from colleagues, so at least I could turn off my webcam and mute myself while I did other things and halfway paid attention.

I planned to meet my friend Jess at a protest after work, so, with my video and microphone turned off, I used the time during the meeting to make a sign. I placed the neon orange poster board next to my laptop on the coffee table and outlined the letters:

BLACK LIVES MATTER

My protest signs usually displayed more creative messages, but I kept this one straightforward. As I colored in the letters, I occasionally glanced up at my laptop, pausing to listen when colleagues said things that were relevant to me.

I glanced over the side of the screen to watch Dakota snoozing in her bucket bed. At this point, she spent most of her time sleeping, but she still kept me company throughout the busy workday. When I moved around, she always followed me: to the kitchen for a cup of coffee, to my office for a meeting, and to the bathroom to keep an eye on me while I did my business. I watched while she did hers, so I guess it was only fair. With a bed in almost every room of our house, she could lie close to me whenever I relocated from the office to the living room, like I had on this particular afternoon.

After an hour, the meeting organizer thanked us all for coming and said goodbye. I turned on my microphone to say "thanks," clicked the red button to end the call, and closed my laptop. The workday was over.

I started getting ready to leave for the protest but took my time since I had plenty. I sauntered down the hall to my office. From the dresser, I picked out a T-shirt and a pair of jeans and carried them into our bedroom to change, putting my dirty clothes in the hamper.

In our tiny bathroom, I wet the bristles on my toothbrush, squeezed out some toothpaste, then wet the brush again because I'm not a monster. With the electric toothbrush buzzing in my mouth, I habitually leaned on the open door behind me and looked to my left. *Huh, no Dakota. I guess she's pretty tired today.*

After I shut off my toothbrush, I heard Brad getting food out of the refrigerator. *He must've just gotten home,* I observed. When I returned to the living room to grab my shoes and protest sign, I noticed Brad's backpack on the bench just up the stairs of our entryway, dropped there when he had come in. I also noticed that Dakota was still in her bed where she'd been lying since my meeting started.

"Hiya," I said to Brad, poking my head in the kitchen.

He was shuffling around from the counter to the fridge and back, making a veggie-burger wrap with his signature set of ingredients: a ridiculous number of condiments. I told him I was leaving for the protest in a few minutes. We talked briefly about how busy his schedule was at work and how the house smelled like permanent marker.

I went back into the living room, slipped on my shoes, and grabbed my keys and phone. Brad sat on the love seat with his dinner on the coffee table. With his iPad propped up on the table, he turned on a clip from a late-night talk show. I was about to say goodbye to him and Dakota when it suddenly hit me. My mind finally processed what my eyes had already taken in: Dakota hadn't gotten up. During all that movement—me getting ready to leave, Brad coming home and making dinner— she was still in her bed.

Something was wrong.

I jumped right into panic mode. Despite the fact that I'm a person who always assumes the best and denies that anything is ever wrong, I was picturing the worst possible outcome. She'd left me on my own to get ready to leave the house, missing her chance to show me that she'd like to come along. Then she'd passed up the opportunity to beg from Brad while he was making dinner. I knew my dog, and this behavior was so out of the norm for her. This was bad.

Wait, I said to myself, trying to stop my thoughts from spinning out of control. *I need to take a step back and be absolutely sure that it's time to panic.* I decided I should investigate further before assuming—or accepting—that the worst pain I could ever imagine might've been closing in on me.

I tried to coax her to stand up. "Dakota, c'mere." Nothing. "Do you want a treat?" Nothing.

She didn't budge. She didn't even look interested. But she didn't look distressed either. She just lay there on her side with her back legs straight against her torso. Her eyes were on me, but her head didn't move from the bed.

She'd had a couple of stumbles that day but nothing alarming. She'd slipped while walking on the living room carpet, which she didn't usually do, but I'd just assumed she had a bit more pain or wobbliness. I just thought she was having an off day. Now I knew it was more than that.

My mind fast-forwarded, trying to predict how this would play out. It didn't feel like dress rehearsing tragedy, though; it felt like actual tragedy. Like a train stocked with everything I'd been afraid of for the past few years was barreling toward me and I was tied to the tracks. I had known it would come for me sooner rather than later, and while I'd thought about it many times, I'd never put it into concrete ideas or visuals. I'd never played the movie in my head through to the end. I guess I'd thought Dakota's mobility would steadily decrease as it had been. I thought we'd make small decisions based on how she was doing each day: whether she was eating and drinking, if she still wanted treats or not, how bad her pain seemed. Instead, here she was, suddenly unable to stand up. It had been over six months since I'd tracked Dakota's quality of life scores. After a few weeks of listing mobility as not so good and everything else as good, it had started to seem like a waste of time.

I looked at Brad with a mixture of helplessness and fear—both from not knowing what to do and, at the same time, knowing exactly what we probably needed to do. Without saying anything, I begged him to tell me what to do.

Brad sat four feet from us, but he was a world away. He was eating quickly and raising his eyebrows. After a busy day at work, he still had work to do that night. He needed to finish preparing a presentation to give at a conference the next day plus log some patient notes from the day's appointments. While I'd gone from zero to *we might lose our dog tonight*, Brad was stuck at a two or three. He wasn't in the best frame of mind to be dealing with canine health problems after a full day of dealing with human ones at the hospital. He was exhausted and just wanted to finish dinner, get his work done, and get some sleep before it started again the next day. But Dakota needed him. I needed him.

We tried helping Dakota up together. "Maybe she just feels weak," I said.

Brad lifted her into a standing position, but her legs remained limp and just buckled. She wasn't even trying to stand up, like she knew any attempt would be fruitless.

My thoughts fast-forwarded again. *How does this end?* Part of me had hope and part of me knew this was the end. All of me didn't want that to be true.

Brad was officially worried too after seeing that Dakota wasn't just *not* standing up, she *couldn't* stand up. I actually found his worry comforting. We were in the beginning of a terrible story, and it would only be more difficult if we weren't on the same page.

Brad and I moved Dakota from her bucket bed to a regular dog bed. But before we did, he put down a pee pad, just in case.

We discussed taking her to the emergency vet clinic. However, that conversation was a short one. She was already weak and frail and old, and we knew that her neurological issues weren't fixable.

Plus, if we took Dakota to a vet, we'd have been putting her through procedures and tests for the best-case scenario of lengthening her life by a few weeks . . . maybe a few months if we were lucky. *But would that be lucky for her?* I contemplated. *More weakness, more pain, more medication that would just knock her out?* I didn't need to think about that question for long. As terrified as I was of losing Dakota, I had to prioritize her quality of life, not my feelings.

I texted Jess to tell her I wouldn't be at the protest because something was wrong with Dakota. She wrote back something supportive.

It took some courage to ask Brad the question: "Do you think we should call Lap of Love?"

He didn't answer. He was in his head, thinking through what we were facing. Wrapping his mind around this sudden reality. Processing.

Brad is almost always the self-assured one in our relationship. He's a doctor. He fixes things. But he usually needs more time than me to process unexpected information.

I don't know how much time passed as I lay near Dakota, crying, worrying, with Brad nearby. Maybe we spoke. I can't remember.

Dakota had been lying down for a while, so we decided to try taking her outside to pee. We attempted to lift her up into a standing position, but her legs still didn't engage. She wasn't able to use her muscles at all. She peed right where we were holding her. Luckily, she was hovering just above the pee pad.

As I watched Brad watch Dakota, I saw the train hit him too. Her complete inability to stand up and her lack of bladder control broke his heart. Mine was already broken. We sat with Dakota for a few minutes, each in our own heads, thinking a million thoughts, both of us stunned and me crying.

I asked again, this time without a question mark: "I think I should call Lap of Love."

Brad agreed.

I clumped down the hall to look up the phone number on my laptop and make the call from my office. I thought that by doing it in a room by myself, I might have an easier time getting the words out without breaking into sobs.

"We take calls until 6:00 p.m.," the recorded voice said. I looked at my phone. It was 6:30.

"If you're calling after hours, we recommend you hang up and call an emergency vet."

As if I needed another heart-wrenching moment. I thought about how we might not be able to do the in-home euthanasia, about how we might have to take Dakota to some emergency vet—in the middle of a pandemic, which meant social distancing. It meant we wouldn't be able to go in with her. I couldn't do that. I *wouldn't* do that.

When I returned to the living room and started to relay to Brad what the voice recording had said, I broke down. He hugged me tightly until I caught my breath.

I called Lap of Love again and left a message, getting out at least a few words before new tears appeared. After leaving a message, I hung up, hoping they'd come through for us. They opened the next morning at seven, so I set my alarm and planned to call them first thing.

At that point, my job was to get Dakota through the night as comfortably as possible. She still wasn't moving or even lifting her head.

"Should we give her an extra gabapentin in case she's in any pain?" I asked. We did.

"I'm gonna run to CVS and get a syringe so we can give her water," Brad said, knowing I wouldn't want to leave Dakota.

When Brad returned, he filled a cup with water and brought it into the living room. Then he gave Dakota some water from the syringe, and she lapped it up feebly. I fetched our biggest jar of peanut butter—one of several with a stick figure of a dog drawn on the lid. I put some on a spoon and held it up to Dakota's mouth so she could lick it.

We stayed with Dakota all evening in the living room. Brad lay on his stomach next to her, his face buried in his arm. He'd later tell me that was when it really hit him that we were losing our girl.

The Night Before

Brad texted a coworker to see if he could cover his work at the hospital. He said he could. But Brad still had to give a presentation the next morning. The chances were slim that he'd be able to get out of it, and he didn't want to ask. My work ethic isn't nearly as strong as his, so, without hesitation, I emailed my boss to tell him I wouldn't be working the next day. I knew he'd support me putting family first. I wished Brad's work requirements were less rigid so he could call off as easily as I could.

He and I decided that he'd sleep in our bedroom while I stayed in the living room with Dakota overnight. That way, he could get some sleep and I'd be there in case she needed anything.

We positioned Dakota's dog bed next to the couch, slid a pee pad under her backside, and draped a light blue towel over her in case she was cold. I kept the syringe and water nearby, as well as the peanut butter and spoon. Brad helped me gather some additional items we might need during the night: a few extra pee pads, a couple of plastic bags for soiled pads, and my phone charger. A little after midnight, Brad hugged Dakota, kissed me, and disappeared down the hall, closing our bedroom door behind him.

I lay on the living room floor next to Dakota's bed. I figured I'd sleep on the couch later, but at that point, I wanted to be as close to her as I could. I texted with Aryenish, my friend who also had a senior dog and who I knew loved her in the same way I loved Dakota. Every dog owner loves their dog, but I considered my love for Dakota—and Aryenish's for Rihana—to be a level above that. These weren't just our dogs; they were our soulmates. I told Aryenish what had happened and that I planned to call Lap of Love in the morning. She sent back empathetic and supportive messages, telling me to let her know if I needed anything. I texted with my mom too. She did the same and told me I was making the right decision. I pet Dakota softly. I told her I loved her. I stared at her. I cried.

When my eyelids started feeling heavy, I moved to the couch. I dangled my arm over the side with my hand resting on Dakota's leg. I tried to sleep but couldn't. Every time I closed my eyes and had a moment to observe my thoughts, I was overcome by a strong desire to look at Dakota's face. I was exhausted, both physically and emotionally, but I was compelled to keep my eyes open so I could stare at her face.

My desire to look at Dakota wasn't new; I'd felt that way her entire life. I often stared at her, took pictures of her, and annoyingly demanded that everyone join me in looking at her. "Look how cute she is." "Watch, watch, watch!"

But this was different. This time, I was keenly aware that my time with her was coming to an end . . . that soon I wouldn't be able to look at her. I tried not to think about that, even though it was all I *could* think about. *Stay present, Lisa,* I told myself.

I put my pillow and blanket on the floor next to Dakota's bed, slid off the couch, and curled up under the blanket. After a few hours of lying by her side, I noticed that a tearstain had formed in the corner of Dakota's right eye. I thought she might've gotten a hair in her eye and I tried several times to wipe it away, but the tearstain kept coming back. I racked my brain trying to figure out what to do to comfort her. I thought for a few minutes but came up empty.

After a while, Dakota began moving her head up and down, maybe an inch. Her nose touched my cheek as if she was nudging me, asking me for help with something. It was one of those things nobody else in the world would've noticed. Dakota had never been a snuggly dog, and she didn't usually like being face-to-face unless I was telling her to give me a kiss, a command she knew might result in a treat.

"What's wrong, Peepers?" I asked, still racking my brain.

I needed to solve this problem for her. I couldn't solve the huge, glaring problem at hand, so I needed to solve this smaller one.

Maybe she'd been lying on her right side for too long and wanted to switch to her left. I'd heard that people who lie in bed for a long time can get bedsores, so it made sense to me that Dakota might've felt sore or uncomfortable after lying on one side for too long. Maybe that was also what was making her eye water.

I decided to turn Dakota over, which is not an easy task when your dog can't move. She wasn't heavy—around forty-three pounds at that point and mostly skin and bones—but she wasn't able to give me any assistance. Her body was completely limp. She seemed so fragile too, and I didn't know if she was in any pain. I didn't want to jostle her or let any part of her drop from my hold.

I managed to lift Dakota's body, so I decided to take the opportunity to see if she needed to pee. Hugging her body against mine with one arm, I quickly slid the pee pad in place with the other. I held her there for a few seconds with both arms.

"You need to go pee?" I waited.

She didn't pee. I was sure she needed to, but I also knew she'd been told for almost fifteen years *not* to pee inside.

I laid Dakota back down on her left side this time and put the towel back over her for warmth. She seemed much more content and fell asleep quickly. I felt so relieved that she was no longer in discomfort. I stayed awake and stared at her.

In the early morning hours, I turned her over again and held her up over the pee pad.

"Need to pee? It's okay, puppy. Go pee."

She peed!

"Oh, good girl! That's a good girl, Dakota!" I made a big show of how proud I was. I wasn't exaggerating.

I slid the pee pad off her bed, folded it up, and replaced it with a fresh one. There was no sign of pee on her bed. No dampness or anything. *Damn, these work well!* I put the used pee pad in the plastic bag nearby.

When I laid Dakota back down, she began moving her tail up and down. Tail pumping! This time, it was a welcomed sight.

She squirmed as much as she could, which wasn't much, but she was desperate not to poop on herself.

"It's okay. Good girl!"

I wanted to lift her up again so she wouldn't get any on her legs, but it was happening too quickly. As she lay on her side and pooped, I braced her body gently and slid the pee pad back, inch by inch, carrying the poop with it, away from her body.

"Good girl, Dakota! That's such a good girl!"

I gathered up the corners of the pee pad, put it in my plastic bag, and tied it shut.

After peeing, pooping, and drinking some water out of the syringe, Dakota slept for a few more hours. She seemed almost content, and I was impossibly happy to know she was no longer anxious or uncomfortable. My world was still shattering, but at least I'd helped her feel better. With a small win under my belt, I was able to doze off.

Around five-thirty the light from the sunrise poured through the bay window. When I opened my eyes, I remembered instantly what day it was: the worst day of my life and the last day of Dakota's.

I could barely let the word *last* enter my conscious mind. Back in January, I had struggled so much to even admit that it might be her last *year*. I couldn't bear to think too deeply about this being her last day.

I rubbed my eyes, attempting to alleviate the sting of exhaustion from crying and sleeping only a few hours. I reached over Dakota to grab the peanut butter and spoon on the coffee table behind her. Then I spooned some peanut butter out of the jar and offered it to her. With each lick, Dakota's jaw made a clicking sound, a sign of how weak her muscles had become. Her breathing was labored, which I hoped was from the extra pain medicine we'd given her and not from pain itself.

I got up and made my way across the house to throw the trash bag outside. Every few steps, through the dining room and sunroom, I craned my neck to see my best friend on the living room floor, at once glad and devastated that she wasn't trying to get up to follow me.

Making Calls

My alarm went off at ten minutes before seven, but I was already awake. Lap of Love opened at 7:00, so I had a little time to muster up the courage to call them. I knew I was doing the right thing, but that didn't make it any easier to say the words out loud. It's funny how we can keep our composure right up until we open our mouths to form the words. Speaking what we feel inside always has a way of making it more real.

"I apologize in advance for crying," I said to the woman on the line. I don't know why I said that. I'm sure everyone cries. "I'm calling to see if you have any availability to come over today." To do what, I couldn't bring myself to say out loud. Sentences end earlier for people experiencing grief.

My heart was in her hands. I needed her to have an appointment for me that day. Dakota couldn't move, and I didn't know if she was in pain. I couldn't take her to a vet clinic and risk not being allowed to stay with her due to COVID restrictions. I needed to be with her, by her side through all of this. For her. For me.

My muscles tightened as I braced for a response from the woman on the phone.

"I'm so sorry, but we're all booked up for today."

I took a deep breath and looked up at the living room ceiling, trying to keep the fresh tears from falling down my cheeks. They streamed down my temples instead, so a lot of good that did me.

In that instant, I dropped my fear of losing Dakota. Discarded it. Forgot about it. It was still there, of course, but it was, if only for a moment, completely overtaken by my fear of not being able to get an appointment, of not doing it at home, of not being allowed to be with Dakota at the end of her life. As much as I wanted to avoid the pain of saying goodbye to her, it was way more important to me to be there for Dakota and do what she needed most from me then. That became my new goal and my previous, contradictory goal—avoid pain at all costs—went out the window.

The woman on the phone quickly offered to send me a list of other services in the area. My head snapped back into place as I looked at Dakota. *Did she just say there are other groups I can call?* It seems silly now, but I had assumed that Lap of Love was my only option. It was the only in-home euthanasia company I'd ever heard of. "Yes! Can you do that?"

"Of course."

I unclenched everything. We weren't out of the woods yet, but we also weren't out of options. I could still get my dog the help she needed that day.

The woman said she'd send the email while I waited on the phone. In normal circumstances, I hate waiting on the phone while someone does something they can do on their own time after I hang up. On this day, though, my impatience also went out the window. I needed that list, and I needed it as soon as possible. If Lap of Love was booked, I needed to call other companies right away in case they were just as busy.

The email appeared in bold at the top of my inbox. Just beneath it were emails about racial justice, a reminder to complete my health profile on 23andMe, and a receipt Dr. Braff's office had sent for the sixty carprofen pills I had ordered two days earlier to refill Dakota's stash.

With tears on my face and a stuffy nose, I thanked the woman and ended the call. The list she sent had about twenty in-home euthanasia companies, and I had no idea how to assess them. It reminded me of choosing a primary care physician every time I've moved. It's a daunting task to pick a doctor— someone I need to be able to trust with my life—based on which name I like best out of a list of names that tell me nothing about their intelligence, experience, or bedside manner. This was even worse. Not only did I have no idea which companies to trust, I also didn't have time to research them or ask anyone for recommendations. I needed to make sure I got an appointment that day.

I clicked on one company and up popped a website that looked like it was created on Angelfire.com in 2004. I returned to the list. After a few more clicks, followed by snap judgments based on web design and not much else, I called Peaceful Day.

As the phone rang, a lump formed in my throat. When I heard a voice, I asked my question: "Do you have any availability for an at-home euthanasia today?" The tears came fast as the word *euthanasia* echoed in my head, and my entire body felt tense as I awaited the person's response.

The woman on the other line—a young woman, judging by her voice—spoke with a warm, compassionate tone. "I think we can do that." I wiped my cheek with my whole palm and rested my hand on Dakota's leg.

The woman never lost the care in her voice as she asked me all the required questions: my name and contact info, what was going on with Dakota, and Dakota's weight and age. I felt like we were in good hands.

She asked for my vet's name and contact information to inform them of Dakota's passing so I wouldn't have to. I noticed that *passing* was a gentle word, and I felt relieved by the woman's detailed kindness. I thought about this later and realize that the woman on the phone had a script I didn't yet have but would soon need to develop.

I was surprised and grateful that the company would take care of informing my veterinarians, but I also couldn't help but wonder if the vets would delete Dakota's records when they found out about her passing. I hoped not. It felt insensitive. I wanted Dakota to live on in every way possible.

The woman on the phone scheduled an appointment for us with a vet named Dr. Green between three and four thirty. But it came with a stipulation that made me cry yet again. The procedure would need to be performed outside due to COVID protocols. I worried equally about the heat and the lack of privacy. It was June in Maryland and the temperature was forecasted to reach above ninety degrees that afternoon, not to mention the humidity. That would be hard on Dakota. Plus, our neighbors' kids had a habit of invading our space when we were in the backyard—shouting over the fence at us while they jumped on their big trampoline. I hated the thought of having to say goodbye to my best friend with them outside playing—or worse yet, watching.

"Where do people usually do it?" I asked the woman on the phone, avoiding putting words to what "it" was. I was afraid she'd suggest a garage or carport. We didn't have either.

"Usually in a garage with the door open or in a carport if you have one." My hand went from Dakota's leg to the side of my face. I squeezed my temples and scrunched up my face. *Dammit.* Putting my hand back on Dakota, I paused to collect myself. This was a problem *we'd* need to figure out. The woman was just doing her job. I read her my credit card information, thanked her, and hung up.

I read through the appointment confirmation email from Peaceful Day: something about the doctor calling with a more exact arrival time, reminders about their COVID policies, and a link to a web page with urns and memorials, which I didn't want to deal with yet. I texted Aryenish, talked to Dakota, and called my mom.

My mom is who I call when I need support, and she never lets me down. She let me tell her all the details of my day thus far. She listened. We cried. Then she told me something she never had before. She said one of her biggest regrets is not being with her dog Rascal at the end of her life. When she had to have her euthanized six years prior, she and my dad had dropped her off at the vet rather than staying with her, because it would've been too hard. Since then, I'd thought about that occasionally and struggled to understand their choice. I couldn't imagine leaving Dakota in her final moments. I mean, I literally could not even picture doing that, at least not without being jailed or restrained or knocked unconscious.

As my mom talked, we both cried. I hate when she's sad, but I also couldn't help but feel grateful to know how she felt and honored that she was sharing it with me. By doing so, she opened a window through which I could gain empathy and understanding. She said if she could do it over again, she would make a different choice. Later, I realized that, in a way, she was. She was making the hard but compassionate choice to be there for me and for Dakota. She was taking a hard-earned life lesson and applying it to support her daughter. Though physically we were eight hundred miles apart, my mom showed up for me emotionally that day and has been there for me ever since.

Wagon

akota seemed in good enough spirits, or at least like she was comfortable. I sat next to her on the floor, thinking about how relieved I felt to have gotten an appointment with Peaceful Day. Another problem solved.

My thoughts shifted to our impending goodbye and how much it would hurt. I caught myself and tried to focus on something else. Logistics. I could handle logistics.

It's gonna suck to wear a mask when the vet gets here. And I hope the neighbor kids don't bother us. I texted Jess to see if I could borrow her canopy, thinking that Brad and I could set it up in the backyard so we'd have some measure of privacy. She said yes, and I made plans to pick it up after Brad got home. I thought about how to make this the best day possible for Dakota. Anytime I'd let myself think about it before, I figured we'd do something to make it fun for her. But I didn't go into too much detail in my imagining. Maybe subconsciously I thought we'd ticked that box already by taking her on the trip to see snow one last time. She had a great last vacation—a whole weekend of Dakota-focused activities.

But here we were on her last day, and Dakota couldn't walk. We could give her some of her favorite treats and shower her with love, but what else? My mind was drawing a blank, but I didn't have the mental or emotional capacity to solve this problem, only to identify it.

As usual, Brad came to the rescue. I got a call from him within minutes. He'd finished his presentation and was driving home. He said it was hard to get through the conference, to concentrate on his speech, to face his coworkers. But he'd gotten through it, and now he could focus on Dakota.

"I'm gonna stop by the store to pick up a wagon so we can take her on a walk," he said.

In fifteen years of marriage, I don't think I'd ever loved him more than at that moment. It was perfect. One last walk for our dog who couldn't stand up.

I lay on the floor with Dakota, grazing my hand over her fur and staring at her face. At one point, I moved her to the couch so she'd have a better vantage point if I had to leave her side to pee or get her more treats. I laid out a soft, white blanket and a pee pad for her to lie on.

I was sitting by her on the couch when I got a text from Brad. The store didn't have any wagons in stock. He sent a picture of a wheelbarrow, followed by the words:

do you think this is safe to put Dakota in for a walk?

Now, listen. I know men want to be thought of as tough guys and problem solvers, and Brad *is* all of that and more. But the sweetness and innocence of his text message brought me to tears and made me so grateful that he's my partner, even in this heartbreaking endeavor. I love him for thinking of buying a wagon, and I love him for his determination to find an alternative when the store didn't have any. If anyone could safely push my frail, old doggy soul mate down the sidewalk in a cart meant for yard waste, it was Brad. But there was no way I would allow Dakota to be pushed around in a wheelbarrow. It wasn't steady or safe. It was too deep and too narrow. Plus, you know, it was bad optics.

I expressed my concerns to Brad without calling him sweet or innocent or typing, "Bless your heart," no matter how badly I wanted to. By the time I texted him back, he seemed to have thought it through as well and changed his mind. He said he would look for a wagon at another store. I told him I'd post on the Nextdoor app to see if any neighbors had a wagon we could borrow in case he couldn't find one.

I stared at the screen on my laptop. I had no idea what to write. I just needed to borrow a wagon for a few hours, but I also needed people to understand the urgency and to know it would be carrying a dog, not a kid. As tears flowed down my cheeks, I typed out a message about trying to take my senior dog on one last walk. By this time, I had quit trying to look or feel presentable in any way, but I wiped my tears enough so that I could see the text on my screen. I kept typing and hit enter. Then I pet Dakota and waited for help from my neighbors.

The kind comments and heart reactions flew in, but nobody had a wagon. A text came in from Brad:

No wagons at this store. Trying another.

Moments later, I heard a knock at my front door. I snuck a peek out the window and saw that it was my next-door neighbor, Marilyn. Though we didn't know each other very well, it wasn't out of the ordinary for her to show up on my doorstep. A couple of times, Marilyn had asked to borrow things like ketchup. Brad and I found it odd because we'd only seen that done on old TV shows. But I liked our neighbors and didn't mind helping them out when I could. Occasionally, one of her sons' toys would fly over the fence and she'd stop by to ask us to toss it back. (Her kids weren't the ones who yelled at us in the backyard. Those were our neighbors on the other side.)

On this particular day, I didn't want to throw back any toys or lend any condiments. I was still in the pajama pants and T-shirt I'd worn all night. I was visibly unshowered, and I'm sure my face was red and puffy from crying and not sleeping much. Plus, Dakota was lying on the couch, and our supplies were strewn all over the living room: towels, pee pads, peanut butter, a syringe poking out of a glass of water, the whole mess. I brushed my fingers through my hair in a half-assed attempt to flatten the flyaway tendrils and threw on a hoodie. Apparently, in this time of panic, I thought that would be an improvement over a T-shirt.

When I opened the door, Marilyn held up her phone to show me the screen. "Is this you?" Her tone was assertive. It barely sounded like a question, more of a demand. It felt parental. On her phone screen, I saw my Nextdoor post about borrowing a wagon.

"Yeah." Tears fell again, and I cared this time. I don't like crying in front of people.

Marilyn offered to lend us her son's big plastic car. "I'll put it in your front yard, and you can take a look and see if it'll work for you."

I thanked her. We chatted for a minute. She was kind.

After a few minutes of sitting with Dakota, giving Marilyn time to bring the little car out front, I leaned out the front door to peek at it. She had told me before that she wasn't a dog person, so it didn't come as a big surprise that the toy was not the right tool for the job. Like Brad's wheelbarrow idea, it was very thoughtful, but it wouldn't work.

So we still didn't have a way of taking Dakota for one last walk. I bit my fingernail. "What are we gonna do, Peepers?"

She kept her head on the couch. I slid my palm underneath it, leaned my head down, and brought her face to my lips. I lingered with my closed mouth on her forehead for a few seconds, then lowered her head to the couch and slid my hand out from under it. When my phone dinged, I snatched it up. A text from Brad. Under a picture of a wagon, it read:

got one! on my way home now

I beamed. "He found you a wagon," I whispered to Dakota, tears gushing down my face.

A few minutes later, Brad arrived, hugged Dakota, and started setting up the wagon in our living room. In the meantime, I threw some water on my face, put on a sports bra, changed into different clothes, and pulled my hair into a ponytail. I hadn't washed it in two days, so it stuck to my head and looked greasy.

When I came back into the living room, Brad had assembled the wagon. It was forest green canvas—a rectangular box with a black, plastic handle. It was also about a foot deep, and Dakota couldn't lift her head, so to make it comfortable for her ride, Brad had put a bed in it, along with some towels for added height and one to act as a pillow for her head. She'd need the extra padding in order to see and smell on our walk.

"When should we take her?" he asked.

"I'll go get the tent first."

After stalling for a few minutes because I didn't want to leave Dakota, I hopped in Brad's truck and headed toward Jess's house, about ten minutes away. She'd left the canopy for me in her driveway before going to work that morning. On my way home, I caught myself driving fast, fueled by anxiety because I knew I was missing valuable time with Dakota. But I'd had all night and all morning with her, and this was Brad's chance to have some time alone with her, so I made myself slow down.

When I arrived, I pulled the truck into the driveway and hauled the canopy through the gate to the backyard. I set it on our deck and went inside to sit with Brad and Dakota for a minute before our walk.

We put the finishing touches on the wagon—fluffing the towels and adding a pee pad—then Brad transferred Dakota from the couch to the wagon while I supported her head and neck. Once we got her situated, Brad pulled the wagon across the living room and through the dining room and sunroom. He carried it down the three steps onto our deck, past the ramp he'd built for her more than a year earlier. He and I lifted the wagon together down the remaining step from the deck to the side of our house by the gate.

Brad pulled the wagon down the driveway and onto the sidewalk toward Loxford Terrace. I followed, making sure Dakota was safe and comfortable. I watched her face, hoping for signs of enjoyment. Her nose wiggled as she sniffed the air. Her eyes squinted in the sunlight. I took pictures and one video, then put away my phone to watch her, unencumbered by devices.

We walked down the hill and turned right onto a road called Malta that led uphill, back to our house. We walked slower on Malta, and Brad and I were both sweating. We stopped under the shade of a tree halfway up the hill, giving Dakota a break from the heat.

We were in the sun the rest of the way home—about five more minutes—and I was a little nervous that Dakota might've been uncomfortable. Brad was too.

Back in the living room, we set Dakota in the same spot on the couch, on her other side this time. Brad brought a fan out from the bedroom and aimed it at her to cool her off. I gave her more water from the syringe and a frozen peanut butter treat to lick. She enjoyed the snack and then drifted off to sleep in the cool air as Brad and I looked on, feeling simultaneously overcome with love yet brokenhearted. Sidney napped in our guest bedroom.

After a while, Brad went out to the backyard, and I stayed with Dakota on the couch. About ten minutes later, he popped his head in through the back door. "Okay, come look out here."

I followed him outside, looking back to make sure Dakota was comfortable. She was still sleeping.

"I was thinking we could put the tent right here." Brad ushered me over to a spot in our yard next to the shed, beneath the trees Dakota loved to scavenge under. I realized that's what he'd been doing outside: looking at our yard, thinking about Dakota, and choosing the right spot for us to say goodbye.

"I like it," I said. It was perfect.

Brad started setting up the tent, and I went back inside. When he was finished, he asked me to come outside again. I was torn, though, because I wanted to stay with Dakota.

"It'll be quick," he assured me, so I followed him to the backyard. The tent was up. On the ground beneath it lay a sheet. A second one hung from the side of the canopy where the afternoon sun shined down and where the neighbor kids would've been able to see us from their trampoline. It was a simple setup and yet it felt like it had taken Brad a while to finish it. He'd put a lot of thought into it, making sure it was perfect for Dakota. And it was.

Brad and I decided to take Dakota on one more walk, a shorter one this time. We loaded her into the wagon again and carried her out the same way through the backyard. As Brad pulled the wagon, I watched Dakota. We stopped halfway, under the shade of a different tree. When I touched Dakota to see if she was warm, I noticed that her hind end and pee pad were wet. "I think she peed," I said with worry in my voice.

"That's okay," Brad said matter-of-factly. "We'll clean her off when we get home."

After I'd reassured Dakota so many times that it was okay to poop inside and then reassured her that morning that it was okay to pee on the pad, now Brad was the reassuring one—both for Dakota and for me.

We switched out the soiled pad with an extra one we'd brought along. I watched Dakota and Brad for the rest of the walk.

It was probably too hot and humid for even our second, shorter walk, but we needed those walks and I'm glad we took them. They were for Dakota, but they were for us too. We wanted to make her last day special. We needed to feel like we did everything we could up to the very end.

Around two thirty, my phone rang with a number I didn't recognize. I answered in case it was Dr. Green. It was. She was on her way. She sounded kind, but I don't remember what else she said other than that I should choose an urn from their website. Talking to her made me feel panicked. She was coming. It was coming.

We'd taken two walks. We'd given Dakota treats. We'd prepared the spot.

At that point, all there was left to do was wait. I felt like I was in a bad dream. I closed my eyes as tight as I could and opened them. *Not a bad dream. It was worth a shot.*

We sat with Dakota, Brad on the couch next to her and me on the floor in front of her. We hand-fed her a bunch of her favorite treats—whatever we had in the fridge and cabinets that we knew she liked. Uncooked, ground Beyond burger; more of the frozen peanut butter treat; Tofurky deli slices; and, of course, peanut butter. In between bites, we gave her water from the syringe.

We reminisced with each other and with Dakota. We spilled the beans to her about all the secrets we'd kept. Fifteen years of coded language. *T-word* means treat; *K-word* means Kong. When we said we were going to take her for a *W*, that meant a walk. I also told her something I hoped she already knew: "You're a good girl."

"The best," Brad added.

By this time, we only had about an hour left before Dr. Green would arrive. On my laptop, I pulled up the Peaceful Day website to choose an urn. I was annoyed that I had to. Online shopping was the last thing I wanted to do in my last hour with Dakota. I wasn't able to articulate it then, but I resented having to choose my favorite out of an array of objects I didn't want. They were all perfectly nice-looking, but they all represented losing Dakota. I didn't want my dog in an urn. I wanted her right next to me, whole and well. Reluctantly, I chose a wooden box with flowers carved on the front. *Whatever.*

"When the vet gets here, I want everything to be set up so we don't have to worry about it." Brad explained his plan to me: We'd meet the vet outside to hear her instructions, then come in to say goodbye to Dakota before bringing her outside for the procedure.

We set everything up before the vet arrived. The wagon, a fresh pee pad, towels, and the masks we were required to wear. We were ready, but we were so incredibly *not* ready.

The whole day felt surreal. Despite the many goodbyes I'd experienced with dogs throughout my life, I'd never actually been present for any of their deaths. This was all new to me. It surprised me that I could feel conflicting emotions simultaneously: heartbreak and gratitude, love and fear.

We had a job to do—to make Dakota's day the best it could be for her and to prepare for the vet's arrival—but the harrowing reason for it all was ever present. Our bodies did mundane things like wake up at a specific time, make phone calls, find and put on clean clothes, but our minds swirled with profound and overwhelming thoughts.

It's probably similar to the feeling of planning a loved one's funeral. It's all new to you, but the actual tasks of what you're doing are so familiar: make calls, visit salespeople, inform family members, choose an outfit. And throughout the process, you hold a core emotion of sadness, but on top of that, there are moments of calm—even happiness—as you think about your loved one and share memories of them.

This was like planning a funeral for a family member who wasn't gone yet. Instead of having to do all the tasks on the tail end of our heartbreak, we were doing them on the precipice of it. I'm not sure which is less awful.

Goodbye #10

For most things in my life, I find myself wishing time would speed up. *I want spring to get here faster. I want it to be the weekend. I want to have been at my job longer so I can leave sooner without looking unreliable on my résumé.* The list goes on.

But on June 4, 2020, I found myself begging the universe for time to slow down. Every new development meant I had less time with Dakota: The vet arrived. Brad met her outside to discuss the plan. Brad came back inside. *Tick, tock.*

"We can take some time to say our final goodbyes and then she'll meet us out back."

That was the part I hadn't let myself think about. Now, I had to.

Brad and I wanted to project happiness and love, to be present for those moments we'd never get back. We knew there'd be time to be heartbroken later. We both tried and failed to keep it together. I sat on the floor in front of the couch, face-to-face with Dakota. Brad kneeled beside us. We each told her she's a good girl, and we pet her and hugged her—tightly but gently. One after another, tears rolled down my face. Dakota gazed at me with her soulful, knowing eyes. I grasped the loose fur on the back of her neck, which I knew I could grip tightly without hurting her.

Brad buried his face in her chest. Her fur was wet with our tears. He kissed her and told her she's perfect. He had the idea to take a final picture of the three of us, him on the right, me on the left, smiling fake smiles through the deep sadness we were sharing. Dakota was in the middle, her head resting on the couch.

I sat back down on the floor and rested my head near hers. I blinked hard.

"Okay, it's time," Brad said gently.

As much as it hurt to hear those words, I didn't resist.

He moved Dakota to the wagon and pulled it through the living room, dining room, and sunroom for the third and final time. We put on our masks, and I moved in front of Brad to open the back door. Dr. Green stood on our back deck, at the bottom of the ramp, waiting to meet us.

Noticing that Dakota couldn't move and had to be carted out in a wagon, Dr. Green offered, "If you prefer, we can do it right here." She gestured toward the sunroom carpet just inside our back door. "We just need to keep the door open for airflow."

Brad looked at me.

"Okay, yes!" We scrapped the plan and the perfect spot Brad had picked out and prepared in the yard. The floor of our sunroom was not a ceremonial spot by any means, but it would be better for Dakota to be inside, out of the heat and humidity, and out of view of the pesky neighbor kids.

Brad and I cleared a spot on the floor. With a big, sweeping motion, Brad moved our pile of shoes out of the way. I wheeled my bicycle to the other side of the room. Brad set Dakota's bed on the floor and covered it with a sheet and a fresh pee pad. Then he lifted her carefully from the wagon and placed her on the bed.

The three of us kneeled around Dakota, Brad and me in front of her and Dr. Green by her back. The vet explained the procedure: Two shots. The first, a sedative. Then the one that would stop Dakota's heart. Brad and I leaned over Dakota, telling her we love her, petting her, and kissing her face. We whispered to her, "You're such a good girl." Words we've said to her a million times.

After that, we'd only get to say them *about* her.

As the vet gave Dakota the first injection, the hugging and crying continued. *I hope she knows how much we love her.*

"Just let me know when you're ready," the vet said after allowing us a moment with Dakota.

Of course we aren't ready. Absolutely not. Never. Get out of our house and forget we ever called you.

Brad looked at me.

"Yeah," I croaked without breathing.

The vet gave Dakota the second injection. Dakota took several more breaths as I squeezed her tighter. After what seemed like ten seconds, someone said, "She's gone." I don't know if it was Brad or the vet. Either way, Dakota was gone.

Ready.

Gone.

That day was full of words I hate.

The vet stepped outside, giving us a moment alone with Dakota. I took off my mask and wiped my cheeks. Brad put his hand over Dakota's eyes for a second, closing them with his palm. I didn't notice him touch her eyelids or apply any pressure at all. I wondered how he did it so gently; maybe I only saw it that way because it was all I could handle.

I traced Dakota's face with my finger. She didn't seem gone. She looked like she was napping. I didn't know that gone and asleep could look identical.

I called Sidney over to us so he could see Dakota. The vet said that, in her experience, cats don't seem to comprehend death, but I did it anyway, just in case. I couldn't tell if he knew Dakota was gone, but he wasn't all up in her face like he usually was.

Brad pulled the edge of the sheet up over Dakota's shoulders. I knew what came next.

He paused.

I pressed my lips together hard.

He covered her head.

I stared at the ceiling and swallowed hard.

"That stung a little," I said, completely lying about the "little" part. It stung very hard. All of this was unimaginably hard.

"I was afraid of that." Brad put his arm around my shoulder and pulled me to his side. We held each other and cried.

Gently, Brad wrapped Dakota in the sheet and picked her up while I supported her head in my hands. Then Brad carried her out to the driveway to the vet's car. I think the vet typically does that part, but Dr. Green let Brad do it—maybe because she knew he's a doctor or maybe because he has the confidence of one. I walked right next to him, not wanting to leave his or Dakota's side.

As we approached the car, the hatchback was already open. Brad laid Dakota down on her side. We adjusted her legs and head to make sure she was in a comfortable position. She couldn't feel comfortable. She couldn't feel anything. We knew that. But we would've punched anyone who pointed that out or tried to stop us. We each kissed Dakota for the last time, then Brad closed the hatchback door, being careful not to slam it. After a heartfelt thank you to Dr. Green, Brad and I stood, wrapped in each other's arms, and watched from the driveway until we could no longer see the car.

Empty

"Now what?" I had a feeling it was a question we'd be asking ourselves and each other for a while. Brad and I sat together on the couch, crying, staring, processing. With Dakota gone, we were lost. We didn't know what to do. Everything was different. The entire world had changed. We didn't know where to look, what to focus on, what to do. Dakota is—was—the center of our lives. Down was up.

The house felt too big . . . empty. Everything inside it was built around Dakota. We chose it in the first place because of its short stairways, which were safe for an aging dog, and its big, tree-lined, fenced-in backyard. We bought it knowing it was where Dakota would grow old and where her mobility would likely decrease.

Everything in it was hers. Not just her beds—one in every room—but the couches we'd bought because the color of the fabric matched her fur. The rugs that covered the slippery hardwood and linoleum floors that we'd purchased when she couldn't walk or stand on them well anymore. Even the cat's litterbox was the kind with a ramp and a lid so Dakota couldn't get into it. She did anyway—daily. She'd stop by the bathroom to check for kernels of litter spilled on the ramp or the floor. That's what I got for buying cat litter made of corn.

The house was Dakota's house—the place where she spent her last few years with us. In early June of 2020, it also became the place where we lost her. I hated it and loved it all at once.

There was no escaping the heartbreak we felt. Nothing we could do would distract us or make us feel better. There was no fixing to be done. We just had to let time do its thing and start to heal our wounds, something neither of us believed was possible amid such crushing pain.

Sometimes when I'm upset, I clean. But I couldn't clean up Dakota's things. Not the regular, everyday stuff, like her beds, her food and water bowls, and her leash. And not the stuff we had out that day: the towels, the pee pads, or the syringe. Not even the wagon, which, over the course of a few hours, had become one of our most prized possessions.

"You wanna go on a walk?" I asked Brad, careful to use the word *on* instead of *for* so it wasn't the exact way I would've asked Dakota. Still, saying *walk* instead of *W* felt strange and sad.

We left through the back door, past the ramps she'd been up and down hundreds of times. I held Brad's hand, afraid to venture out into unknown territory. Yes, it was my neighborhood, where I'd walked hundreds of times. But it suddenly existed in a world without Dakota. A world I didn't recognize. A world I didn't belong in.

We encountered a couple of neighbors with their dogs, and, surprisingly, I was glad to see them. It would've made me miss Dakota if missing her wasn't already a constant feeling. Page, a friendly neighbor we saw occasionally, passed by with one of her little dogs.

"How's your pup doing?" she called across the street. She didn't know anything about what we'd just been through. She was just asking to be nice, probably noticing that we were walking without Dakota, which was unusual. I didn't know what to say. I didn't have my script figured out yet. I hadn't thought about how to answer that question. The only words I could think of would've made me cry, and I didn't want to cry. So I let Brad do the talking. He hesitated too, then said, "She passed." I could tell he kept his answer short to avoid crying.

Page replied with something neither of us could make out, so we smiled half smiles and kept walking. I ended up seeing her again a few days later, and once again, she asked how Dakota was doing. It occurred to me then that she hadn't heard Brad before, so I had to tell her Dakota had passed away.

Brad and I didn't talk much on our walk. But we weren't crying either, and that was a nice break. We just held hands and put one foot in front of the other.

A bunch of components were missing from my bedtime routine that night. I didn't give Dakota any pills. I didn't give her a kibble of cat food when I filled Sidney's automatic feeder. I didn't take her outside for one last pee before bed. I didn't shine my flashlight on her bed to watch her lie down and make sure her whole body made it onto the bed. I just brushed my teeth, put on pajamas, and lay down next to Brad, who was already in bed but not yet asleep. As if it wasn't enough that he'd given a presentation that morning, he had to work a full shift the next day. Dakota had passed on a Thursday, and I was off work until Monday.

Through the darkness, I stared up at the ceiling. I closed my eyes for a few seconds at a time. They burned with exhaustion. But my mind wouldn't let them stay closed. I couldn't go to sleep in my bed as if my world hadn't just blown up. It felt too normal—too much like something a person does when everything's fine. I didn't want to act like everything was fine. I didn't want to go to sleep without Dakota there, and I didn't want to wake up without her. Going to sleep felt like acceptance. I did not accept that Dakota was gone.

I left the bedroom and went out to the couch. I sat backward, leaning my chest against the back of the couch, resting my chin on my folded arms, and watching out the window as the trees swayed back and forth during a late spring rainstorm. I pretended that Dakota sent me the storm to keep me company in my sadness. I've had to say goodbye to so many dogs throughout my life, but it's really painful to recount those times, so I don't. With Dakota's passing so raw and present, I didn't have the luxury of time or distance or childhood ignorance. That goodbye was right in front of me, and I couldn't *not* think about it. It consumed me.

Being Dakota's person was who I was and the void I felt without her had robbed me of my identity. I cried and missed her and fought off sleep until I couldn't anymore.

Words and Pictures

Thursday, June 4, 2020, was Dakota's last day. Friday, June 5 was my first day without her.

I woke up alone. Brad had left for work. Sidney hadn't come over to me for morning snuggles. After rolling over and seeing Dakota's empty bed, I flung myself onto my back and stared at the ceiling. When a tear trickled down my temple, I pressed my lips together, and, using all my willpower, I hoisted myself up from the couch. Nobody followed me into the kitchen or the sunroom. Nobody needed to go outside. Nobody needed pills.

Our supplies from the day before were still strewn around the house: Dakota's food bowl, her bed in the sunroom, the wagon full of towels. I didn't feel any pressure to clean them up or get rid of them. They'd stay right where they were until I was ready to move them, whether it was later that day or later that year.

I leaned over the wagon, picked up the towel that Dakota had lain on the day before, and examined it for the first time. It was thick and fluffy and pale blue made even lighter by fading. I don't even know where we got it. But suddenly, it was precious.

I held the folded towel up to my nose, closed my eyes, and breathed in the smell. Dakota's ears and feet had that wonderful aroma dogs have—like a mixture of corn chips, syrup, and dirt. I knew that Dakota's smell would soon fade from this towel, her beds, our lives. I worried that I wouldn't remember it. I took another whiff, concentrating hard to commit the smell to memory. Then I placed the towel in the wagon and walked back into the living room.

I fell onto the love seat and pulled my laptop from the coffee table onto my lap. I entered my password and waited while the screen loaded, watching the little circle rotate clockwise. Everything was moving forward, but I didn't want to.

I thought about Brad at work and how impossible it must've been for him to be there. I grabbed my phone off the coffee table and texted him:

i love you

In the midst of my feelings of loss, of nothing making sense, there was one thing I was more certain about than ever: I'd picked the right life partner. Brad has been all in for me and for Dakota—from her first day with us to her last. He'd served as the voice of reason when she started aging and I didn't want to notice, when I thought surgery would be a cure-all for her problems, and when he knew we should take her to see snow before it was too late.

We had both assumed Brad would be the strong one at the end, keeping his composure while taking care of everything that needed to be done. Sad inside but outwardly stoic. He *did* take care of things—like finding a wagon and making plans with the vet—but emotionally, he was just as much of a wreck as I was. In fact, on top of being heartbroken about losing Dakota, Brad had been fighting the urge to blame himself—for getting irritated when she had accidents in the house, and for not being able to somehow prevent her passing. Leave it to him to feel guilt over not being superhuman.

I didn't want Brad to feel any blame or have any regrets. But his visible grieving over losing Dakota made my own a little easier to face. It didn't hurt any less, but it made me feel understood and supported to be with someone who was hurting as much as I was. Grief expert and author David Kessler said, "Grief must be witnessed." Brad and I had witnessed each other's joy and love for Dakota for fifteen years, and then we'd witnessed each other's equally enormous grief. I sent another text:

a lot

I tried writing a post on Facebook to tell my friends that Dakota had . . . that we'd had to say goodbye. I typed. Revised. Deleted all of it. Nothing did her life justice. Nothing did my pain justice. But I needed to share something. Grief had crashed down on us, leaving our little world in rubble. I wanted the world outside our house to be impacted too.

I kept it short and simple, but it still made me cry. I'd share a better tribute later, when I was more capable, less broken. I hoped that time would come sooner rather than later, if at all.

The comments and reactions to my post came flooding in. In a matter of minutes, I discovered how much words matter in times of grief.

The past tense broke my heart:

> Dakota was . . .
> Dakota had . . .

And the one that stung the sharpest:

> I know how much you loved her.

As if not only was Dakota gone, but so was my love for her. As much as words could hurt, they could also help. The present tense, the shared sense of loss, and the specificity that showed that people cared—that they would remember her:

> I never even met her, and I could feel your deep, sincere, and never-ending love for Dakota.

> I don't often cry over other people's dogs, but you were so kind to share her with us all these years, and now I'm sitting here on my sofa just trying to hold it together.

> I loved seeing you love her through photos and videos. The dog bed that often got stolen by a certain cat, the way she'd only sit in it halfway, getting to know her backyard, chomping on carrots, going on her special weekend away. She clearly was, and is, a sweet and special soul.

As the comments continued to roll in, I read each one immediately and thought about how loved Dakota is—by me, of course, but also by all the people who knew her in real life or through my social media posts about her.

I thought about how I'd shown up for others when they'd been grieving and about the many times I hadn't. I'd used the past tense. I'd left generic comments. Sometimes it was to show support to a person I wasn't that close with. Other times, it was because I cared a lot but had no idea how to convey that—or was afraid to.

I thought I knew how much they were hurting. I thought I could understand. I mean, I'd lost family members before—all my grandparents were gone. I could imagine losing Dakota, but I really had no idea what it felt like until I actually felt it.

Before I decided not to have kids, my mom used to say something that annoyed me to no end, partly because it was a cliché and I don't like clichés, and partly because she said it a lot. Too much. Like, once would've been fine. If I ever expressed any judgments about how she or anyone else parented or interacted with their children, my mom would say, "You can't understand until you have kids of your own." She only ever said it about parenting, but I think it applies more broadly. I thought I understood the grief that comes with a dog passing away, but I didn't until I'd experienced it firsthand. I had to go through it myself. I guess my mom was right. I hate when that happens.

I thought about where I was when my parents said goodbye to Rascal: probably reveling in my new job in animal rights, but not translating that compassion into being as supportive as I could've been for my parents, whose hearts were breaking. I'd failed again when my mom lost her parents, one after the other. I thought a lot about my mom's loss: how much she'd done for her parents as they aged; how the world isn't fair because she doesn't deserve to feel sadness; how shattered I would be if I lost her. But I don't think I was there for her, physically or emotionally. I thought back to my grandpa's funeral in Tennessee—and my awkwardness at his funeral. I didn't know if what I was feeling was what I *should've* been feeling, and it made me uncomfortable and exposed to let my emotions show.

The people in my life have always shown up for me when I've needed them. Atop that list are my mom and Brad. After losing Dakota, I wondered if I'd done enough to show up for them—or even to let them show up for me. I hold back. I fight to be seen as independent and carefree. I keep a lot of worries and anxious feelings bottled up. I made Dakota into a crutch for my own insecurities. Her company was always enough to comfort me and ease my pain so that I didn't have to address issues directly with the person involved. If I had Dakota, I'd convinced myself, I had everything I needed. It wasn't until after I'd had to face the reality of no longer having her that I was able to be fully vulnerable with others—that I've been able to let them see me.

I was glad that I'd been fully present on Dakota's last day— for her and for myself. I didn't worry about being vulnerable. I couldn't be anything *but* vulnerable. The same was true the day after. I spent the morning being jolted back and forth between feeling okay and feeling crushed again. But this time, I didn't judge any of it; I just let it happen.

Looking through pictures of Dakota made me smile and laugh. I cried when I dropped my phone on the floor and instinctively looked at Dakota's bed to see if I'd woken her up. I smiled as I grabbed a few baby carrots—one of Dakota's favorite snacks—from the fridge. And I sobbed because the crunch of my first bite reminded me of her eating them just a few days before.

Every time I left a room, I thought about helping Dakota up so she could follow me or trying to sneak out so I wouldn't wake her. Every time I entered a room, I had the urge to say, "Hi, puppy." Those things had become second nature; I did them without thinking. But a split second later, my conscious mind would kick in and register that Dakota wasn't there.

Part of me hoped those automatic reactions would stop soon. They hurt so bad each time. The other part of me hoped they'd continue. I hated the thought of Dakota not being part of my life every day, and at least with those subtle reminders of her, she still was.

I shared those thoughts with my friend Sara, who'd lost both of her dogs over the past couple of years. She recommended that I maintain my routines to ease the grief. For example, if I usually talked to Dakota, I should still do that. I took her advice. After using the restroom, I walked into the living room, looked at Dakota's empty bed, and said, "Hi, puppy." When I went out back, I said, "Let's go." It felt silly, but it helped.

As the influx of Facebook comments and messages slowed, I spent most of the day looking through pictures of my life with Dakota. I had started the night before, actually, finding old photos in my phone or in recent Facebook albums and showing them to Brad or texting them to my mom. Alone at home with my grief, I went back further—as far back as the start of my Facebook account. I've had the account since 2005, so loading all the pictures was not a speedy process. I also looked through

Instagram, an account I'd opened in 2013. I even considered accessing my old Myspace account, but I'd tried that several years earlier and it had crashed my computer, so I didn't risk it.

What started as reminiscing turned into a passion project: I decided I'd find all the pictures I could and save them on my computer so they'd be in one place. I needed something to fill my time, but all I could think about was Dakota, so this was perfect. I spent hours clicking and saving pictures to a folder called "Dakota."

After realizing I had hundreds of photos and experiencing so much gratitude even at this low point of grief, I decided to make them into a photo album to keep forever. And, let's be real, to also make everyone else look through them any chance I got.

In my office closet, I found a stack of CDs that I'd burned photos onto back in my twenties. When Dakota was a puppy, I had a nice digital camera, so those pictures are big and high resolution. I opened each one and zoomed in to see the details of Dakota's face: her youthful, golden fur, her paws, her eyebrows.

It was weird seeing pictures of Dakota when she was young, doing things that we'd deemed dangerous in her later years: jumping, rolling over on her back, using stairs, and even sitting! She didn't sit anymore once she got old. My guess is that it no longer felt comfortable for her. Those times seemed so long ago that I could barely remember what they were like. My friend said recently that when someone lives long enough, it's like they're two distinct individuals: the young version and the old version. That felt true as I reminisced about Dakota's fifteen years.

I worked on the photo album every day for several hours—finding photos, organizing them, choosing which ones to put in the album, creating the pages. By the time I finished, ten days after Dakota's passing, I'd collected more than 2,500 photos. I found an album online that came standard with twenty pages. If I needed more than that, I could add two additional pages for $2.49. I added thirty-six pages.

Visitors

The weekend after Dakota passed, Brad and I cried, reminisced, and supported each other. When we couldn't bring ourselves to go to bed, we slept in the living room together. We took walks and discussed grief and vulnerability and what tattoos we wanted to get to honor Dakota's life. We bonded over how much losing her hurt. It *physically hurt*. I knew people said that but it didn't sink in to me how true it was until I experienced it for myself. My chest, neck, and jaw felt tight, and my eyes and brain were exhausted from the stress and overuse.

On one of our walks, Brad and I decided to go into the woods near our house. As soon as we entered, we saw three deer. That's not uncommon, but it felt different. The deer in the back of the group, the smallest of the three, came closer to us than deer usually do. She seemed interested in us and had an expression on her face like she was thinking, *Hey, do I know you two?* Brad half joked that she was Dakota reincarnated. I took her picture and included it in the photo album.

Losing Dakota forced me to face big questions about my identity. For fifteen years, I'd been her person, her best friend. I'm a dog person. I'm Dakota's person. That identity had intensified during her final two years as she aged and began needing more care. I was home with her all day, morning to night. She was the sun in my little universe. *Who am I now without her?* I wondered.

I'd left the job that had me stressed all the time and taken the job that gave me better work-life balance and still let me work from home. But that job wasn't my passion, and without Dakota there, all the reasons I had for keeping it were crossing themselves off the list. So I started thinking about what I truly wanted out of a job. I also started writing again. First, I made lists: Dakota's favorite foods, words that Dakota knew, places she'd been, and so on. Then I started writing down my memories of her life and her death. I wondered if I could find a job that involved more writing.

In the days after losing Dakota, the emptiness of not having a dog in the house weighed on me. I felt lonely and aimless. I called my mom during work breaks but had nothing to say. I looked at blonde dogs on Petfinder.com and wondered what it would be like . . . if it was even a good idea. *There's no way I could ever love another dog as much as Dakota.*

A week after we said goodbye to our girl, we invited our friends Dave and Angie over for dinner. They had just moved to the area from Washington State, and Brad was eager to welcome them to the East Coast. I was happy to see them and even more excited to see their dog, Wilson. He was a senior like Dakota.

The day of their visit, Brad and I worked hard to straighten up the house. The shutdown and our loss of Dakota had the place looking even rougher than usual. We ran the robot vacuum cleaner, which we'd named Hairy years ago since most of what it picked up was pet hair. We shoved things in drawers and closets. We wiped the counters. Around two o'clock that afternoon, I heard the slam of the metal lid on our porch mailbox. The mailman had come. When I saw what came that day, I didn't know if I should laugh or cry. In the rusted black mailbox sat a small white package that read:

Wisdom Panel: Essential Dog DNA Collection Kit

I had forgotten that I ordered it two weeks prior. My eyes blurred as I reached in and grabbed the box. Thinking about Dakota hurt terribly but I still wanted to. Having her in my mind and experiencing the pain it brought was far better than trying to push her out of my thoughts. That felt like a betrayal. I liked reminders of her, and that's what the DNA test was.

I didn't have time to deal with the kit right then. We needed to straighten up the house before our guests arrived, but neither Brad nor I knew what to do with Dakota's stuff. The wagon, the towels, the beds—everything was still where we'd left it a week before. "You can do whatever you want with it," Brad told me. "You can leave it right where it is. You can put it away. Whatever you're comfortable with."

All I could bring myself to do was move things toward the walls so they'd be out of the way. I wheeled the wagon from the middle of the sunroom to the wall between the dining room and sunroom. I left Dakota's bed on the sunroom floor, next to the pool table.

Later, Brad grilled veggie burgers while I sat nearby at the patio table with Dave and Angie. The three of them made conversation, and I chimed in when I wasn't focused on Wilson. His fur was black with gray streaks throughout and tan markings on his face and front legs. He was sweet, regal, and had fantastic eyebrows. It was comforting to have a dog at the house again. He used the ramps in our backyard, and Brad brought out one of Dakota's water bowls for him to drink from. When some neighbors set off a firework—yes, in June—Wilson began pacing. "He doesn't do well with loud noises," Angie said. "He was shot with a BB gun before we adopted him."

"Oh no! Should we take our food inside?" I asked.

Brad added, "Yeah, we can go inside."

"Sure, if it's not too much trouble," Angie replied, sounding grateful.

We were happy to accommodate an old dog again. We sat together at the dining room table, eating and reminiscing. I was still preoccupied with Wilson, watching him amble around our house, smelling where Dakota had been.

But when Wilson sniffed Dakota's bed, my hackles instinctively went up. Smiling and trying to look as if I were completely comfortable with it, I watched him. As silly as it sounds, part of me felt protective over Dakota's bed, over her scent, over what we had left of her. I tried to quiet those thoughts and focus on the stronger ones—the ones telling me that Dakota's bed was helping another old dog.

I gazed at Wilson while he snuggled up in Dakota's bed, finding comfort where Dakota once had. Sidney sauntered out from the bedroom to meet him, perhaps to see if this old dog would take an interest in his butthole. Wilson lived with three cats, though, so he wasn't impressed. He looked at Sidney, then set about licking the bed in true elderly dog fashion. I laughed and felt grateful.

The next day, Brad put Dakota's wagon in his truck, and we dropped it off at Aryenish's house. She and her partner, Kenny, started using it every evening to walk with their old dog, Rihana.

That evening, I mustered the courage to ask Brad, "Do you think we'll adopt another dog?" I didn't think he'd be ready to talk about that—or even to think about it hypothetically. I assumed that, to him, considering adopting again would feel like a betrayal of his loyalty to Dakota. He's big on loyalty, which is probably why he sticks with me even though I do things like bring up adopting a dog when I know he's probably not ready.

"Ever? Of course," he responded. "I think we'll always be a dog family."

Dang it. I forgot to include a time frame in my question. Any good fundraiser knows to include specifics when making the ask! Apparently, I've gotten a bit rusty.

"What about soon?" I asked, smiling to cover my nerves.

"Really? I'm surprised you're ready to think about that."

"Me too," I confessed. "But I think I am."

Forever

The next week, I pulled into a parking spot near the door of the vet clinic. I stayed in my car, following the COVID-19 rules for social distancing. In the next parking spot, a man sat in his truck, presumably waiting to pick up his dog after a vet appointment. He probably assumed I was there for the same reason. He had no way of knowing the real reason I was there.

I called the clinic phone number on my car's Bluetooth and actually spoke without crying. *Whew.* I was tired of crying. I was still a total wreck over losing Dakota, but I was also eager to get her back in a way. I thought about the man in the truck and how we should all treat each other better since anyone we encounter might be going through something painful.

I wondered how it would feel to hold Dakota's ashes. Friends and acquaintances had told me it would be comforting. I didn't believe them. Yet, when I'd received the call an hour prior, alerting me that her ashes were ready to be picked up, I dropped everything and drove straight there. I told my boss I had to run an errand and was finished working for the day—at three in the afternoon.

I watched a vet tech bring a black dog out from the clinic. The man in the truck stepped out to open the door of his extended cab, and the dog jumped in. *Good, not the truck bed.* The guy backed up and pulled away, and the vet tech went back inside. I waited.

A woman in a mask and scrubs walked out of the building, carrying a gift bag. *My turn.* I pulled my mask up over my nose and mouth and pressed the button to open my window.

I vaguely remember the woman being kind. If she said anything to me, I don't remember. I was focused on the bag in her hands. As she passed it through my open window, I grabbed it, thanked her, and closed the window.

The bag was made of dark blue paper and had a straw handle. I opened it, took everything out, and set it all on the passenger seat of my car: a folded paper, a small cardboard box, and the hand-carved urn I'd reluctantly chosen just five days before.

I decided to save the ashes for last.

I opened the folded paper first. On the bottom, it read:

This certificate will serve as notice that Dakota was cremated by Pet Memorials this 6th Day of June, 2020 as an expression of your gratitude for the unselfish devotion and companionship your pet shared with you.

I couldn't help but notice that the date was two days after Dakota had passed away. For a split second, I thought about her body waiting somewhere to be cremated, being handled as if she were an object. I quickly made myself think about something else.

I picked up the little cardboard box and opened it. It held an off-white ceramic mold of Dakota's paw. Without taking it out of the box, I felt the contours of the imprint with my fingers and started to cry. Later, I showed it to Brad and cried again because I couldn't answer his question about which of her paws it was. *Left? Right? I should know my best friend better than this!*

I closed the box and placed it on the seat. With both hands, I picked up the urn, which was inside an opaque protective sleeve. I set the sleeve on the seat and admired the urn. I had forgotten what it looked like since I'd seen it on the Peaceful Day website. It was beautiful: a wooden box, a little smaller than a box of tissues, made of mahogany or something similar. A tree, maybe a cherry blossom, with slender branches and flowers with round petals was carved on the front. I hadn't looked at it in as much detail when I'd picked it out.

I slid open the lid, curious to see the ashes. I'd never seen ashes before, a human's or a dog's. I hoped there would be enough to scatter some, use some to make ink for a memorial tattoo, and keep the rest forever. When I opened the box, there they were, in a clear plastic bag, zipped closed at one end. A rush of thoughts and feelings and questions flooded my mind, hitting me all at once.

There are more ashes than I thought there'd be.

How is this my dog? How is this my best friend?

There are some bigger pieces. I'd find this to be gross if these were anyone else's remains.

This isn't my dog! My best friend, with all her spirit, could not be reduced to fragments that can be zipped up in a plastic bag.

People were wrong. I don't feel comforted holding these. It's heartbreaking to have ashes instead of my best friend, alive and well.

At the same time, they were right. *I do feel comforted. I know nothing.*

I lost a lot when I lost Dakota: the dog of my life, my best friend, my identity. People who've met me since she passed don't know me as Dakota's person. They don't get to meet the girl I spent every day with for fifteen years, the girl I shaped my life around, the girl who made me *me*.

But I still have so much. I have the love we shared. I have the lessons she taught me about being present, about acceptance and equanimity, about living life to its fullest and finding joy wherever I can. I have fifteen years' worth of memories—in photos, in my writing, in her ashes—that I wouldn't trade for anything.

I've taken every morsel from our epic love story, and I carry Dakota with me in everything I do. I've started writing again, mostly about her. I go for walks and listen to sad music and think of her. I sing along to "Winter" by Bayside and cry a mix of sad and joyful tears. I see her in every deer, every falling leaf, every tree that sways in the wind. I left the job I wasn't passionate about and launched my own business with Dakota's face as the logo and her spirit as the inspiration. I try to be a better wife, a better daughter, sister, and friend. And sooner than I ever could've guessed, a better dog owner to another golden-brown puppy with adorable eyebrows who needed a family as much as we needed her.

I've become a lifeline for friends and family members when they find themselves confronted with difficult goodbyes. I've taken what my loved ones did for me and paid it forward. I try to say the right things. I've brought them food and ordered them wind chimes with their pups' names engraved on the wood. Most of all, I understand their pain, so I offer my shoulder and my support. I tell them they can talk to me anytime—day or night—the day after they lose someone or ten years later. I tell them there's no expiration date on grief.

I might not get to massage Dakota's scruffy neck fur anymore or help her up from her bed or see her smile in the sunshine. I might not get to sit on the deck with her or take her to the dog park. But she will remain a huge part of who I am.

When I picked up the protective sleeve to put the urn back inside, I noticed a silver nameplate taped to it with Dakota's name engraved on it. "Oh yeah," I said to myself, remembering that I'd had the option to include the years of her birth and death. I'd opted not to. She was Dakota and always will be Dakota, and there's no end date to that.

Ashes or not, keepsakes or not, I'll carry her with me for the rest of my life.

My best friend. My Dakota. My Peepers.

She's not going anywhere.

Acknowledgments

Heartfelt thanks to:

- Dakota, for being my soul dog and the best good girl;
- Brad, for supporting—nay, championing—this project;
- Phoenix and Sidney, for the breaks, laughs, and snuggies;
- my family (especially Mom, Dad, Chip, and Karla) for always being there for me;
- my proofreaders, beta readers, and writing friends: Kim Gonsalves, Jocelyn Cox, Emily St. Marie, Leah Patriarco, (Aunt) Stormy Harrison, Erin Gaines, Jennifer Gordon, Kate Green, Mary Ellen Kearney, Stuart McDonald, Theresa Schmidt, Mimi Stevinson, Jeannie Trizzino, Christopher Locke, Anneliese Kamola, Gretchen Primack, Nick Leydorf, Ashley Schnepf, Kendra Thompson, Mary Keever, Lauren Lanier, Julie Taylor, Isabella Warner;

- my cover designer Robin Ridley and cover illustrator Rachel McGuire; and

- my copy editor Jennifer Huston Schaeffer and manuscript reviewer Sabine Sloley.

About the Author

L isa Rimmert began her career in marketing, public relations, and fundraising in 2006. She holds a bachelor's degree in mass communications from Southern Illinois University Edwardsville and a master's in public relations from Webster University.

Lisa is a member of the Dog Writers Association of America, the Independent Book Publishers Association, and Women Funders in Animal Rights. Her work has been published on TheBark.com, and, as a stand-up comedian, her jokes have echoed through bars and comedy clubs all over the United States.

This is her first book.

Find out more at www.LisaRimmert.com
or by following Lisa on social media @lisarimmy.

About the Publisher

In addition to authoring this book, Lisa Rimmert owns and operates On The Nose, LLC, the publisher of this book. On The Nose helps people and organizations change the world through effective communication. We love words. We write them, edit them, publish them, and empower others to use them effectively. While our specialty is communicating about animals and their well-being, we've also successfully:

- helped a solar nonprofit share knowledge that's advancing energy rights for all;
- crafted compelling emails that raised money to feed the hungry and shelter the unhoused;
- edited educational materials that are training activists worldwide; and
- empowered individuals to stand out on their quests for their next careers.

Learn more at www.OnTheNoseComms.com.

Made in the USA
Monee, IL
12 May 2023

33577437R00163